CHRISTIANITY AND THE DOCTRINE OF NON-DUALISM

A MONK OF THE WEST

CHRISTIANITY
AND THE DOCTRINE
OF NON-DUALISM

Translated by
Alvin Moore, Jr.
Marie M. Hansen

SOPHIA PERENNIS

HILLSDALE NY

Originally published in French as
Doctrine de la Non-Dualité et Christianisme
© Éditions Dervy–Paris 1982
English translation © Sophia Perennis 2004
First English Edition 2004

Series editor: James R. Wetmore

For information, address:
Sophia Perennis, P.O. Box 611
Hillsdale NY 12529
sophiaperennis.com

Printed in the
United States of America

Library of Congress Cataloging-in-Publication Data

Moine d'Occident
[Doctrine de la non-dualité (advaita-vâda) et christianisme. English]
Christianity and the doctrine of non-dualism / a monk of the West;
translated by Alvin Moore, Jr., Marie Hansen.—1st English ed.

p. cm.

In English; translated from French.
Originally published: Doctrine de la
non-dualité (advaita-vâda) et christianisme.
Paris: Dervy-Livres, c1982
ISBN 0 900588 82 9 (pbk: alk. paper)
1. Advaita. 2. Vedanta. 3. Hinduism—Relations—Christianity.
4. Christianity and other religions—Hinduism. I. Moore, Alvin.
II. Hansen, Marie M. III. Title.
B132.A3M6613   2004
261.2'45—dc22   2004019469

cum permissu superiorum

The I-AM has sent me unto you.

Exodus 3:14

CONTENTS

PREFACE

AT THE VERY END of this short but profound book, the author has this to say about his 'Christian Vedānta':

> As for ourself, we will say unequivocally that after more than forty years of intellectual reflection on this doctrine, having allowed it to impregnate us more and more profoundly, we have found nothing that has seemed incompatible with our full and complete faith in the Christian Revelation.

By way of introduction we shall endeavor to provide some context for the author's uncompromising interest in the Vedānta and his equally uncompromising Christian loyalty.

In principle Christianity is a *bhaktic* esoterism, to which its very forms abundantly testify; in practice it is an exoteric religion of love. It is an esoterism, providentially called upon to fulfill the rôle of an exoteric way for a considerable sector of mankind. It cannot be, however, that this providential rôle excludes esoterism and *gnosis*, for a sapiential path is implicit, *mutatis mutandis,* in every orthodox tradition, however few may be called to follow it, and our Christian tradition cannot be uniformly categorized at the level of some lowest common denominator. Every orthodox religious tradition contains within itself *in potentia* the full spectrum of spiritual possibilities open to mankind, and to be fully human entails the recognition of these possibilities; for man has no right to be content with less than the highest that is open to him. But not everyone is endowed with equal acuity of vision, nor with equal capacity to understand. In Christianity, as someone has aptly said, the esoterism-exoterism dichotomy can be usefully conceived on the analogy of a sliding scale. The separation between the esoteric and exoteric orders is more a matter of degree than of kind, both the esoterist and the exoterist sharing the same doctrinal foundation but understanding it in differing degrees. The differences result from the wayfarer's innate capacities (a lack thereof can often be compensated by perseverance), his desire to know, his penetration, and the understanding that derives from this; but the differences are real. There are those whose penetration and understanding remain undeveloped because they are absorbed in more ephemeral interests, because they neglect the sacrifices which *gnosis* demands. The heart, as intellectual organ, does not know unless the entire creature yearns to know. Ultimately, since only God can know God, 'whosoever knows God becomes God'. Our knowledge of God—a *gnosis* to which all are bidden, each in his degree—is God's knowledge of Himself through man as instrument.

A commonplace of Western medieval Christendom was the dictum, 'Christ revealed what Moses veiled.' It is argued that with the birth of Christianity the exoterism-esoterism dichotomy has been abrogated, that this is taught precisely by the rending of the veil of the Temple. This is true in principle, but it is far from true in practice. Christian thinking, especially in its post-Reformation phase, has moved steadily away from anything that might lead towards gnosis. Almost without exception, the individual is deemed a finality; individual, social, and institutional interests are paramount. Man is no longer effectively understood as a deiform creature, a *capax Dei* whose penultimate Subject is the Logos. In practice he is conceived as little more than a body somehow endowed with a measure of consciousness. Further, in its inveteration Christianity has become the most structured of all extant traditions, often organized in the manner of secular government bureaucracies: elaborately staffed chanceries with departments of this, that, and the other—all unwitting testimony to the forgotten truth that the Kingdom of God cometh not with organization. Metaphorically 'tithing mint and dill and cumin', we neglect 'the weightier matters of the law, justice and mercy and faith' (Matt. 23:23). A serious pursuit of these weightier matters demands the employment of our best faculties in 'seeking first the Kingdom of God' (which in the final analysis is God Himself), the penetration of doctrine, discernment between the essential and the non-essential, a mercy that considers the needs of the inner as well as the outer man, man's postmortem destiny and ultimate destination, and faith, which, as an intellectual virtue, has no upper limit. To be as just as possible, however, it must be noted in passing that Christ came not to abolish but to fulfill the law and that He enjoined a certain attention to detail, saying, 'These ye ought to have done and not to have left the other undone.' (Matt. 23:23) But He also severely reproved those who neglect the pursuit of gnosis and who hinder those who, in spite of everything, have a sapiential vocation: 'Woe to you, lawyers, you have taken away the key of knowledge. You have not yourselves entered in, and those who would enter you have hindered.' (Luke 11:52)

There is, however, an aspect of necessity in the present sapiential desiccation of Christianity, for, like all else under the sun, the great trends of Christianity, at least in their outer aspects, are subject to the laws that govern all existence. The existentiation of the possibilities of creation entails objectification, centrifugal movement, movement away from the Principle. It is in the nature of things that man must objectify before he can interiorize. Revelations and other divine initiatives towards mankind that are manifested in the formal order answer to this innate human tendency towards exteriorization. Nevertheless, the innermost thrust of the tradition is towards the Interior. 'Seek ye first the Kingdom of God....' (Matt. 7:33; Luke 17:20, 21), which is within. We are from God and must return to Him.

This, then, is a conceptual map and characterization of the cosmic moment in which *Un Moine d'Occident*, 'A Monk of the West', as he signed himself for purposes of this book, would live out the path he followed, a path which led to his writing *Doctrine de la Non-dualité et Christianisme,* of which the present work, *Christianity and the Doctrine of Non-Dualism,* is a translation. The author, who later used the transparent pseudonym of 'Elie Lemoine' (Elias the monk), was a lay brother (that is, a professed monk though not a priest) of the austere Cistercian Order. Alphonse Levée (his name in civil life), was born at Paris in 1911; his father was a skeptic, his mother a devout Catholic. His secondary education was at a commercial high school, and he did the usual compulsory military service. In 1935 he went to Indochina for a short assignment on behalf of a Parisian commercial house. In 1938 he returned to Indochina for another Paris firm, but this time he was caught up in the events of World War II and had to remain in Indochina until 1946. He was again in the Far East in 1950 and 1951, this time at Singapore. Around the age of twenty he came upon a copy of René Guénon's *Orient et Occident* (*East and West*) at a second-hand book stall, and he describes[1] how he found this discovery dazzling and numinous—*ce fut un éblouissement!*—and indeed, it marked him for the remainder of his life. He corresponded with Guénon and though this correspondence was cut off by the War, it was undoubtedly influential in his decision to pursue a monastic vocation in a contemplative order, a decision taken in principle when he was about thirty years old. His vocation was delayed, however, because he had become the sole support of his mother. But she died in 1951, and later the same year he entered the great Abbey of La Trappe, the mother house of the OCSO, the Cistercian Order of the Strict Observance. At La Trappe he lived for decades in quiet anonymity, though judging from what is known of his later years his interior life was anything but idle and unfruitful.[2] He became thoroughly familiar with the works of St Thomas Aquinas, with the Church Fathers, especially those in favor in Latin Christianity, and among these latter especially St Bernard of Clairvaux (whom Catholics consider the last of the Fathers). And he continued to study works pertaining to the Vedānta, those of Guénon as well as the Hindu authorities on this *darshana,* notably Shankara. It is worth noting that when he became a Trappist he inevitably brought with him considerable conceptual baggage derived from years of studying Guénon and the Vedānta. He was not asked to jettison this—which would hardly have been possible—but was allowed to pursue these interests and even encouraged to do so.

The French original of the present work was originally published with the permission of Brother Elias' monastic superiors and with the encouragement of several clerics, among them a responsible theologian and a Vatican cardinal. The original edition carries the subtitle: *jalons pour un accord doctrinal entre l'Eglise et le Vedānta—*

---

1. Many of these details are taken from Brother Elias' obituary in *Études traditionnelles,* no. 514, October–December, 1991; others from the preface by Jean Tourniac to the French edition of this book.

2. During this time, two of his books were published, *Doctrine de la Non-dualité et Christianisme,* 1982, and *Theologia Sine Metaphysica Nihil,* 1991. In his later years he wrote regularly for *Études Traditionnelles* and served as editor of the journal.

'landmarks for a doctrinal accord between the Church and the Vedānta.' Our author finds no incompatibility between the most orthodox Catholic doctrine as set forth by St Thomas Aquinas, and the Vedānta as interpreted by Shankara, the premier Hindu exponent of the *Advaita* (non-dualism). This is the more notable in that Brother Elias is intellectually rigorous both in his understanding and use of St Thomas' teaching and in his handling of the Hindu sources. Perhaps this is the place to express our only *caveat* regarding the book, which indeed may be no *caveat* at all. But it has to do with the subtitle; if a Christian esoterism is to be revived before the end of the present dispensation (and we believe in this likelihood), it will not be by borrowings from the Vedānta, from Sufism, or even from the Kabbalah, or indeed from any other extra-Christian tradition. A *jñānic*,[3] or sapiential, esoterism is intrinsic to Christianity, which is in the nature of things; it cannot be grafted on from without in any effective manner. Rather it must be actualized once again by the rediscovery of its roots, in Christian scripture and doctrine, in the Liturgy, and in the works of figures such as St Dionysius the Areopagite, John Scotus Eriugena, Meister Eckhart, and Dante Alighieri, among others; and above all in Christ Himself. Brother Elias does not urge any kind of impossible amalgam between Christian doctrine and the Vedānta. His concern is rather to demonstrate that the most orthodox interpretation of Christian doctrine is in no way in conflict with the Vedantic doctrine of non-dualism, and that a comparative study of extra-Christian sapiential doctrine can be of immense benefit in reawakening an understanding in depth of Christianity's own doctrinal resources. It is to the great credit of certain leaders of the Cistercian order that they had the perspicacity to permit Brother Elias to follow the promptings of the Holy Spirit in this direction.[4] In any event, we believe that he would agree with our

---

3. This Sanskrit word is cognate with the Greek *gnosis*.

4. At least two French houses of the OSCO have demonstrated a notable intellectual perspicacity. There is La Trappe and the ambience it provided for Brother Elias' work, and also the Abbey of Bellefontaine which for years has been publishing ascetic and mystical texts of Orthodox Christianity. Can we see in this a recognition that the predominantly affective Catholic spirituality which had prevailed since the Counter-Reformation has been found wanting?

conclusions, and that his predilection for the Vedānta was entirely as it should be and was never intended to supplant his Christian allegiance, which it obviously did not. It was a choice dictated by personal circumstances as well as those of time, place, opportunity, and above all by Providence.

There are a few last considerations to which we wish to call attention. We have seen that a primary resource of Brother Elias is the official theology of the Roman Church, which he handles faithfully and masterfully. It is noteworthy that, in his understanding, this theology is in no way opposed to an adequate understanding of the Vedānta such as an orthodox Vedantin might entertain. One must not conclude, however, that Thomism, even generously understood, is crypto-Vedānta—it functions from a very different perspective— nor that it provides the only route for a Christian approach to non-dualism. There is, for example, the major doctrine of exemplarism, a doctrine which, though present in St Thomas' writing, is understood in a diminished Aristotelian sense. More often than not neglected, exemplarism is nevertheless strongly implicit in the third petition of the *Pater Noster*: 'Thy will be done on earth *as it is in Heaven*', and is essential to the iconography of Orthodox Christianity. But within the whole body of Christianity, it is perhaps most explicit in the *Divine Comedy*, where Beatrice represents Dante's archetype[5] or exemplar *in divinis*, and where she has a truly axial rôle throughout the *Comedy*. Ananda Coomaraswamy describes exemplarism as 'the traditional doctrine of the relation, cognitive and causal, between the One and the Many.' According to traditional exemplarism, the eternal reality of any and all phenomena necessarily remains within, *in divinis* (cf Exod. 25: 9, 40), while what we ordinarily assume to be real, ourselves included, is rather a web of ephemera and appearances. The Meaning of meanings is not to be found in *this* world nor in any of its prolongations, nor anywhere in the cosmos, but only in the metaphysical order.

ALVIN MOORE, JR.

5. One must on no account confuse Jungian 'archetypes' with divine archetypes. The former are at best perverse caricatures of divine ideas.

FOREWORD

We hesitated for a long time before deciding to publish the present work, which first occurred to us back in 1964, and which was virtually complete a number of years ago. Certainly, it would never have reached this point without the goodwill and encouragement of Fr Étienne Cornélis, to whom we willingly submitted it on the kind suggestion of Cardinal Marella, then President of the Secretariat for Non-Christians. After having read the work, Fr Cornélis generously wrote to us,

> I have a positive appreciation for its fundamental content, for I consider it a serious and sincere contribution to the search for the truth of things . . . and I offer you my best wishes for its suitable completion, to the advancement of religious dialogue and the theology of religions.

'The truth of things'. Indeed, this is what we have sought before all else. We do not consider it astonishing that a study of this kind should come from a contemplative monk. In truth, before being a composition destined for publication, it was first, and in essentials remains, a free and personal meditation to which the interior life of the author is committed, and were it not for the spiritual significance of this work, it would never have seen the light of day. The work touches on something so fundamental that, in this day of the 'meeting of religions' (an inexhaustible source of challenges and questions), it is no longer possible to ignore or pass over it in silence. In this connection we would like to mention the testimonies of two people whose personalities carry particular weight. One, which is already thirty years old, is from Fr Daniélou, then not yet cardinal:

Who knows whether the future of contemplation and the renewal of monasticism are not to be found through the mystical powers of India?[1]

The other, a little more recent, is from Fr Congar:

On the strictly theological plane, dialogue has not yet progressed very far. Now, however, theology has left the schools to encounter other systems of thought, and this may take it a long way. Our own conviction, reached after some twenty years (and here summarized), is that we cannot avoid the quite radical appraisals coming from other wayfarers, who initially were so often neglected or refused: the questions of the Christian East, posed for nearly fifteen centuries, and perhaps those of the Orient as such.[2]

Beside the question of truth is the scarcely less important question of opportunity,[3] and in this regard, present circumstances in the life of the world and of the Church—the queries, uncertainties, and general questioning which have arisen almost everywhere and in every field—seem (without failing in prudence or charity) to justify the spread of ideas which are assuredly perilous for insufficiently mature or unstable minds. Moreover, we believe that a frank and clear exposition of problems is always preferable to a multitude of poorly founded opinions which can only sow trouble and disorder.

The idea of a 'Christian non-dualism' did not originate with us. It appears that Vladimir Lossky first used the expression to characterize Meister Eckhart's doctrine, writing,

Meister Eckhart tries to express dialectically what he says elsewhere in terms of a doctrine of analogy: a vision of the unity of

---

1. Jean Daniélou in *Centre catholique des intellectuels français*, 1949. *Foi en Jésus-Christ et monde d'aujourd'hui: Semaine des intellectuels catholiques* May 8–15, 1949 (Paris: Flore, 1949).

2. Yves Congar in *Centre catholique des intellectuels français*, 1966. *Réflexion chrétienne et monde moderne 1945–1965*. Paris: Desclée de Brouwer.

3. It is no doubt accidental that the first words of the Conciliar *Declaration on the Relationship of the Church to Non-Christian Religions*, are *Nostra Aetate* ['Our Generation'; these two words constitute the title of this declaration. TRS]

being which is not a pantheistic monism, but rather a Christian 'non-dualism', appropriate to the idea of the creation of the world *ex nihilo* by the all-powerful God of the Bible—'He who is'.[4]

The spirit in which the present work was undertaken is well expressed in a pertinent observation made by Fr Cornélis, which we take as our own:

> Their preoccupation with apologetics (on the part of most West-ern authors who write about Eastern spirituality), generally viti-ates their attempts at understanding, and despite the ardor brought to the debate, the problem which first motivated their interest remains unresolved.[5]

When our work has been read, we believe that the reader will bear witness that our sole concern has been *to understand*.

Finally, a declaration from the Secretariat for Non-Christians freed us from the last scruples that we may have had regarding the publication of the results of our investigations and analyses:

> He [the Christian] will refrain from *a priori* rejecting as neces-sarily and wholly monist and non-Christian, the ideal of identifi-cation with the Absolute which dominates Indian spirituality (*tat tvam asi*: thou art That, that is to say, the Absolute) and Muslim mysticism (*ana'l-Haqq*: I am the Real—God, Hallaj).[6]

Given the primarily spiritual perspective that has guided this work, and in which it should likewise be read if the meaning and scope are to be grasped, we have not considered ourself obliged to employ the transcription of Sanskrit terms used by specialists, for we are not a specialist in any degree or in any way.

---

4. Vladimir Lossky, *Théologie negative et connaissance de Dieu chez Maître Eck-hart* (Paris: Vrin, 1973, 2nd ed.), p263.

5. Étienne Cornélis, 'Spiritualité chrétienne et Spiritualités non-chrétiennes', *Concilium: revue internationale de théologie*, p75, n9.

6. 'Vers la rencontre des religions, Suggestions pour le dialogue', *Bulletin du Secrétariat pour les non-chrétiens* (June 1967) supplement. Cf. *Documentation Catholique*, n1502 (October 1, 1967), col. 1663.

1

PHILOSOPHICAL MONISM
AND
NON-DUALISM

UNTIL RELATIVELY RECENTLY, orientalists and theologians agreed that the teachings of the Vedānta, and particularly the 'doctrine of non-dualism' (*advaita-vāda*), were simply monism and pantheism. An isolated exception was Fr Fallon, who in 1954 wrote:

> Shankara . . . the greatest scholastic of medieval Hinduism, was a philosopher and a contemplative who penetrated very profoundly into the mystery of the divine Absolute, the transcendent Self which constitutes the deepest stratum of our being.[1]

However, in 1965, several months after the visit of Paul VI to Bombay, Dom Henri Le Saux, who had been a colleague of Abbot Monachin,[2] published a position paper on the question of 'Hindu pantheism' in the review *Carmel*, and this no doubt had some repercussion on the later development of relations between India and the

---

1. Pierre-qui-Vire, France (Benedictine Abbey), *La Priere*. Témoignages: cahiers de la La Pierre-qui-Vire, no. 43 (Paris: Desclée de Brouwer, 1954).

2. Abbot Jules Monchanin, a priest of great intelligence and erudition, went to India in 1939 in fulfillment of a long-standing interest. Initially he served under the Bishop of Tiruchirappali, Tamil Nadu. He was joined in 1948 by Dom Henri Le Saux, who adopted the Indian name 'in religion' of Swami Abhishiktananda, 'He whose joy is the anointed of the Lord', i.e., Christ. In 1950 the two founded the Saccidananda Ashram on the banks of the Kaveri River near Tannir Palli, Kulittalai District, Tamil Nadu. TRS

Church (the Document of the Secretariat for Non-Christians cited in the Foreword dates from June 1967):

> In the West [wrote Dom Le Saux], regarding the faith not only of essayists but even of renowned writers, Indian thought is very often considered as irremediably engaged in monism and pantheism to such a degree that its integration in Christian theological synthesis seems absolutely out of question. We are sorry to disagree with these authors, but the authentic tradition of India is neither monist nor pantheist, at least not in the sense in which these words are currently understood in the West. Nevertheless, we do not deny the monist or pantheist tendencies underlying certain Indian systems,[3] nor do we deny the frankly monist or pantheistic deviations of certain modern authors. Simply put, we ask that the thought and the spiritual experience of India should be judged according to authentic sources and the Masters and Sages[4] of universally recognized worth.[5]

In this introductory chapter we will attempt to do no more than seek *an* understanding of the Vedantic doctrine of 'non-dualism' which can be accepted by Hindus faithful to their own tradition, but which will also not be adverse to insertion into a Christian perspective; this is to say that to some degree the point of view adopted here will aim at mutual concurrence. We say *an* understanding, because it is known that 'Hinduism has never had the organic, ecclesiastical, and dogmatic unity of Christianity' (Fr Fallon), and this allows it to accommodate itself rather freely to a great multiformity while maintaining its own spirit. Naturally, to be able to pronounce the authentic Hindu tradition exempt from pantheism, we must understand this word according to its precise meaning, since, according to Dewey, 'the term has a wide and loose meaning especially in

---

3. 'System' should be understood as *darshana*. See chap. 7 for the exact sense of this word.

4. Whenever possible, we retain the capitalization and italicization of the original. TRS

5. Henri Le Saux, [no title given], *Carmel*, 1965, no. 2, p120, n18. On Dom Le Saux, see M-M Davy, *Henri Le Saux, Swami Abhishiktananda, le Passeur entre deux rives* (Paris: Cerf, 1981).

controversial writings, where the *odium theologicum* attaches to it; in this way, it is used to denote almost any system which transcends current or received theism. . . .'[6]

As the doctrine of non-dualism represents an aspect of Indian intellectuality and spirituality which, despite everything, is still rather unfamiliar to the European mentality, we shall try to introduce it by a Western text. As simple point of departure, we shall take several lines from St Bernard, who, among the Western Christian masters not suspected of heresy, seems to us to be the man of spirituality and the Church doctor whose position on this point most closely approximates that of the Vedānta. Moreover, he was taxed by some of his contemporaries with pantheism, and in our view this parallel is not without significance.

We could also have started with 'Dionysius', but his authority (the authority of whom?) has too little backing, and his profound thought is almost as ignored as that of India, and indeed some of his views seem to suggest the influence thereof. Thus we have *Esse omnium est, quae super esse est deitas*[7] (It is the Being of all beings, this Deity which is above Being). Nor do we speak of Eckhart, 'so audaciously Platonic that he appeared to be pantheistic—and still does in the eyes of many,'[8] and whom no one from the Catholic camp would seriously dream of taking as a foundation for *rapprochement* between India and the Church, whatever the laudable efforts undertaken in our day to establish his orthodoxy. We will cite him occasionally.[9]

---

6. Cited by André Lalande, *Vocabulaire Technique et Critique de la Philosophie*, entry for *Panthéisme* (Paris: Presses Universitaires de France, 1976), p734.

7. Pseudo-Dionysius, *Celestial Hierarchy*, chap. IV, cited in the Latin commentary of St Thomas Aquinas [no publication information given. TRS].

8. Joseph Marechal, *Études sur la Psychologie des Mystiques*, vol I, 2nd edition (Bruxelles: l'Édition universelle, 1938), p216.

9. It should be noted, however, that in spite of the profound differences between the two men, Meister Eckhart's doctrine of God is very near that of St Bernard: 'While it would be too much to say that the fifth book of the *De consideratione* formed Eckhart's doctrine of God, the evidence indicates that he found in it a valuable traditional resource for some of the most important aspects of his teaching.' Bernard McGinn, 'Saint Bernard and Meister Eckhart', in *Citeaux: Commentarii cistercienses*, XXXI, 1980, p377.

Quid item Deus? Sine quo nihil est. Tam nihil esse sine ipso quam nec ipse sine se potest: ipse sibi, ipse omnibus est, ac per hoc quodammodo ipse solus est, qui suum ipsius est, et omnium esse.[10]

Again, what is God? That without which nothing exists. It is as impossible for anything to exist without Him as it is for Him to exist without Himself: He is to Himself as He is to everything, and thus, in a certain way, He alone is who is the very Being of Himself and of everything.[11]–

We shall shortly return to the *quodammodo.* St Bernard does not say absolutely that things are not, but 'in a certain way'. Monism is excluded. Conversely, he does not limit himself to stating that God is the Being (*Esse,* and not *Ens*) of Himself and of everything, which would be *qui ipsius est, et omnium esse*; he specifies the very Being (His 'own Being'), *qui SUUM ipsius est, et omnium esse.* Again we reiterate. St Bernard does not say that God is the Being of Himself (genitive) and of all, which would be *qui SUI ipsius est, et omnium esse,* but that He is the very Being (nominative) of Himself and of all. *In other words,* SUUM *qualifies* ESSE *both as Esse of God (*IPSIUS*) and of all (*OMNIUM*).* To our knowledge there is nothing in all of unmistakably orthodox Catholic tradition which, even in expression, approximates this point concerning the Vedantic doctrine of the Supreme Self (*Paramātmā*).

Here, it is true, an objection could be made. Is it really legitimate to attribute such scope to a simple word of which the use is perhaps quite naturally explained by a certain relaxation in composition which would certainly be quite understandable in a written work of such sustained effort? This is easily dismissed when we recall that the discovery of subsequent editions has revealed a constant concern on the part of St Bernard to express his thought with the most extreme precision possible. Moreover, it goes without saying that

10. Bernard of Clairvaux, *De consideratione*, v, 6, 13 [no publication information given TRS]. The resemblance with Dionysius will be noted (Migne, *Patrologia Latina*, 182, col. 796).

11. The author translates literally from the Latin. A looser, but perhaps clearer, translation might say: 'He is His own existence, just as He is existence to everything, and so in a certain way, He alone exists who is His own very existence and that of everything.' TRS

the supposition of pantheism on the part of St Bernard, doctor of the universal Church, is likewise excluded. In these circumstances, how are we to understand this *suum esse*?

Here we should recall a common sense observation made by Fr Mersch.[12] If it is an error to consider true what is outside the limits of the truth, it is no less an error to consider false what is within these limits. There is no neutral zone separating truth and error, no sort of no man's land into which entrance is forbidden. Truth extends as far as error itself, while excluding error. And without doubt, when it is a matter of requirement and the sphere of God, do we not usually go to the very extreme frontiers of truth? 'The sum of our words is, He is all.'[13]

This is the very heart of the mystery—and of the paradox—of creation, that while the creature must be said to be and in reality is distinct from the Creator, essentially as well as existentially, nevertheless there is no more being (singular) if creation is included than if it is excluded. It must be noted, however, that in order to speak of an essential distinction, the word 'essence' must be understood according to its common philosophical meaning where, conjointly with the word 'existence', it designates what defines and distinguishes each being of the created universe. In a 'Platonizing' perspective this term admits of a transposition conferring on it a sense very close to that of the 'divine Ideas', notably with St Augustine, where they appear as the Archetypes *in divinis* of all existents. Understood in this way, it must then be said that the essence of beings is not really distinguished from the divine Essence itself. As we shall see below, this was the position of Nicholas of Cusa and, of course, Meister Eckhart.

---

12. Émile Mersch, *La Théologie du corps mystique*, Paris: Desclée de Brouwer, 1954, vol. 1, p93. Cf. Yves Congar, *Vraie et fausse Réforme dans l'Église* (Paris: Cerf, 1950), pp246–247.

13. Eccl. 43:29. [Unless otherwise noted, all passages are taken from the Douay Version. TRS]

There will always be an outlook that emphasizes distinction, and another that accentuates the absence of addition, and this is certainly quite legitimate on condition that neither ever lose sight of the complementary aspect. But in general those of one outlook will always tend to suspect heresy among their opposites. In this case, however, we have an additional particularity: when one of these viewpoints has hardened and become exclusive, it leads to a characteristic heresy, pantheism; it is not so with the other viewpoint, whence the temptation to lean towards the surer side, for it does not seem that the hardening on the part of the created *esse* is properly heretical provided its origin *a Deo* is maintained. Nevertheless, if we conceive of the creative act as entirely in the past, thus making the present *esse* of the creature belong absolutely and exclusively to itself (but *who* possesses?), a tendency all the more seductive in that it is compatible with appearances and 'common sense', then we are left with a merely verbal profession of the dogma of creation; we will then not reach the fullness of truth, and are thus led almost unfailingly to see pantheism in everything that lies beyond.

In reality, the created *esse* is the property of God in a twofold sense. First, not only as related to past origin, but at present; then—and especially—not in virtue of a simple legal appurtenance but by the very nature of things, and, if one dare say so, in its very being of being. Here, we believe, is the explanation of the *suum esse* of St Bernard. The creature does not belong to himself, but all save the intelligent creature are ignorant of this. We emphasize: this is true first of all of his free acts themselves which are certainly personal and responsible acts, but in no way his own acts, being also—we should say being first—acts of God, the universal First Cause. In reality I have as my own only the interior act by which I adhere to evil recognized as such. This is mine, totally and exclusively, and it is a profound mystery. It is nonetheless true that God does everything, because evil as such has no *being*, and 'everything that happens is worthy of adoration.' Is the abandonment of this 'archaic' concept of causality (which must not be confused with 'occasionalism' such as that of Malebranche), always the consequence of moral refinement, as is claimed today? As for us, we see in this rather the sign of a progressive individualization, which is nevertheless providential.

This is still more profoundly true, then, of our existential core itself, *of our existing as person.* Being properly pertains to God,[14] *suum ipsius, et omnium esse*: it does not belong to me to be who I am; he who I am is not I; I am not what I am. The renowned divine 'definition' of Exodus will have been recognized, but as inverted. The 'world', of course, can only see alienation and scandal in this doctrine, and this is natural, *because it is precisely the alienation of the true man which constitutes the 'world' as such.* We will recall that for St Bernard, the world was the 'region of dissimilarity'. Had he lived in our day, he would have added, 'and of alienation'. The 'quest for the Self' (to use different terminology) seems to us to be central in his spiritual doctrine. Let us add that the latest developments of modern thought already make this reaction seem out of date. Today the world would gladly say that to this point we believed that religion alienated man, but we now understand this was not so, and that in reality the idea of God created the idea of man, faith in God faith in man, in brief, that the illusion of God created the illusion of man; and thus we now understand that *man is not.* Here we think especially of a certain structuralist trend or of some cybernetic conception. It is Marxism turned inside out and surpassed (revealed!). It is also man's annihilation (which at the time was promised to come about in millions of years), now replaced by his simple nonexistence. Is this the collapse of all our reasons for acting, as Teilhard thought? In any case, today we clearly see that the *Alliance between God and man is constitutive of Man.*[15]

True man is *actually* (in the twofold sense of presently and effectively) relative to the Creator-Agent, and this actuality of the relationship which places him in existence, makes him essentially an image of God. As Étienne Gilson profoundly observed, 'Image—the greater man's resemblance, the more he is himself.' This very traditional doctrine of the image is central for the knowledge of these things. It introduces us directly to the Hindu doctrine of 'cosmic

---

14. Cf. *Summa Theologica*, IaP, Q 13 [especially a11. TRS].

15. Cf. John Paul II, 'The manifestation of man in the full dignity of his nature cannot take place without reference to God, both conceptually and existentially,' *Dives in Misericordia*, 1,1 (Paris: Édition du Centurion, 1980), p 22.

illusion', *Māyā*, a doctrine too often disfigured and poorly understood, sometimes in the East as well as in the West.

We are familiar with the traditional Indian image of the sun reflected in the waters of the sea.[16] The sun, high in the heavens, is the transcendent and immutable Principle;[17] its reflection dancing on the waters ceaselessly breaking up and reforming, is contingent being, which by turns appears and disappears. This image allows us to set forth the doctrine of non-dualism in simple but nevertheless sufficiently precise terms, at least as an introduction, which the following chapters will complete and refine.

As the reflection of the sun in the water is illusory with regard to the real sun although in itself it is a real reflection, so the contingent being is illusory with regard to real (divine) Being although in itself it is a real contingent being. And just as all the reality of the reflection comes from the real object without which there would be no reflection, so likewise all the reality of contingent being comes from real (divine) Being without which there would be no contingent being. Just as the reflection of the sun is at once real and illusory, so contingent being is both real and illusory. If we attempted to isolate the image from the object and to reduce it to itself, it would immediately cease to be, *since it is solely the actual relationship to the real object which makes it a real reflection*. Take away the object, and the reflection has already disappeared. Thus the world understood as the totality of existents is simultaneously reality and illusion (*māyā*), *reality in itself*, illusion with regard to the Supreme Reality in which everything that has any reality participates and without which there

16. Cf. René Guénon, *L'Homme et son Devenir selon le Vedānta* (Paris: Éditions Traditionnelles, 1978), pp59–60.

17. Contrary to what might be thought, this term is not alien to the great Catholic tradition if understood in the sense here given it, as is testified by these words of Pope St Gregory the Great: *in contemplatione, principium, quod Deus est, quaeritur* (in contemplation, one seeks the Principle, which is God). *Moral.* c.37, cited by St Thomas, *Summa Theologica*, IIA IIAE, 180, 4, *sed contra*).

is nothing whatsoever, *sine quo nihil est.* It must be understood, however, that nothing is illusory in itself. *The illusion is entirely in the one who takes the reflection for the sun itself, or the world for Reality; Illusion is Ignorance.*

If we place ourselves at a slightly different point of view, we can say further that the world is both identity and distinction, identity because, since the reflection of the sun is not other than the sun (reflected), so too the world is not other than Being; and distinction because, as the reflection of the sun is not the real sun, so also the world is not Being. Non-dualism is thus spoken of in a double sense. First, in the sense that, despite the multiplicity of reflections, there are not several suns but one only, remaining unaffected by the multiplicity of reflections; and then in this sense, that each of the indefinitely multiple reflections, even while not being the sun, is, however, not other than the sun, as it is entirely constituted by the radiation of the latter. *Entificum lumen* [life-giving light], we would readily say, borrowing from the prologue to the *Rule of St Benedict.*[18]

It should be clear that the sea or the waters enter into the symbol only as a condition extrinsic to the reflection, which is itself the essential element. We have here only two 'realities' (which, moreover, do not make two), the sun, quasi-absolute reality (we will see the reason for this qualification further on), and the reflection, 'prescinded' from the waters which bear it, a reality that is entirely relative to the first, what Nicolas of Cusa expressed in particularly happy terms:

> Is there a man who might understand that a single infinite Form might be diversely participated in by various creatures, although the creature's being cannot be anything other than the reflection itself of this Form, not really received on a real screen, but diversified in a purely contingent manner? It is as if an artisan's production, dependent on the intention of the artisan, possessed no other existence proper to itself than that of this dependence whence existence comes to it, like the image of a face in a mirror

18. The exact phrase in the prologue to the *Rule,* is *deificum lumen* (deifying light). TRS

that of itself is nothing, either before or after receipt of the image.[19]

Harphius, a fifteenth-century Flemish mystic, wrote:

The wheeling sun is an essential light sending forth its rays everywhere without undergoing any diminution; and though it does not communicate the essence of light to its rays, nevertheless it gives these rays an eternal contiguity which maintains them in existence in such a way that at the moment this contiguity disappears, the very being of the ray disappears completely. Just so the soul, which flows forth from the abyss of divinity, preserves a certain continuity with its origin in which it is maintained and nourished, and which it desires above all else to seize and to enjoy.[20]

In Islam, a slightly different image is used, that of a mirage in the desert. This symbol, which is also found in India, is more adequate in that the support of the reflection is more tenuous (air instead of water), thereby rendering the symbol more vivid, but it also lends itself more readily to the danger of pantheism, or it would do so if the Islamic communities were not still more hermetic than their Indian counterparts, but what filters out from these Islamic confraternities immediately hardens into heresy.

What we have just said of the world in general can also be said of man. He is himself at once reality and illusion, reality in himself, illusion within regard to the Supreme Reality whence all his reality proceeds and without which he would not exist. Again, like the world, man is both identity and distinction, identity because, just as the reflection of the sun in the water is not other than the sun (reflected), so man is not other than Being; and he is distinction because, just as the reflected sun is not the (real) sun, so man is not (divine) Being, which is the Reality of realities (*satyasya satyam*). There is, however, a capital difference between the case of man and

19. Nicolas of Cusa, *De Docta Ignorantia,* chap ɪɪ, in *Œuvres choisies de Nicolas de Cuse,* trans. by Maurice de Gandillac (Paris, Aubier-Montaine, 1942), pp 107–108.

20. Cited by Louis Cognet, *Introduction aux Mystiques Rhéno-Flamands* (Paris: Desclée, 1968), p 299.

that of other existents: alone in his world—which is one of the pos-sible 'planes of reflection' of divine Light—and by reason of the cen-tral position he occupies therein, man is directly called to union (*yoga*) wherein the Delivered (*mukta*) realizes or, more precisely, verifies—for there is no change—the illusory or entirely dependent character of his existence, '*having no other being of its own than this dependence*' of the human individual *vis-à-vis* the Supreme Self (*Paramātmā*), which is true and total Being. Rather, it is Beyond Being, entirely free from every condition of limitative determina-tion whatsoever: *Ipse solus est, qui suum ipsius est, et omnium esse . . . quae super esse est deitas* (He alone is who is the very Being of Himself and of all beings, Deity beyond Being).

We have just said that, like creation, Deliverance is not a change. Indeed, Shankara teaches that it is not the 'production of a non-pre-existing result.' Nor is it an *experience* of the psychological order; no experience of It is possible, because what is 'illusory' (in the above sense, which in no way implies 'docetism'), *is not simply the body, it is the human composite in its entirety.* This observation permits us to understand the error of those who would see idealism or subjectiv-ism in Vedantic doctrine. From the perspective of the non-dualist, the 'mind' (and especially *my* mind), is as illusory as 'matter'. Here we have a capital intellectual and spiritual point: *the soul is not the Self.* We shall revisit this. In India, the concept of cosmic Illusion, or of divine manifestation, plays a role analogous to that of creation in the West, and it has *an equally broad application.* We must now pause at some length on this point.

It seems to be generally accepted that every doctrine endeavoring to go beyond metaphysical dualism but lacking the concept of creation can only end in pantheism. In our view, this is a prejudice, which we would like to try to demonstrate. We can gauge what is involved if we recall that the idea of creation, which is of Hebrew origin, is not found outside the 'Abrahamic' religions, Judaism, Christianity, and Islam. To accept this opinion, therefore, is *ipso facto* to consign to pantheism all that is alien to this group.

It will not be inappropriate to begin by recalling just what the notion of creation is, for it is much less simple than might appear at first glance. We follow St Thomas, whom we cite once for all.[21] To create is properly to make something from nothing, *ex nihilo*. But what does this mean? There are several ways to understand the preposition *ex*. It may simply indicate an order: where nothing existed, there is now something, and this sense is legitimate in this context. It can also signify that from which things are made, and this sense is to be rejected. God has not made the world *of* nothing, as a mason makes a wall *of* bricks. *Nothing* is not the material from which creatures are made. *Nothing* is not anything. Finally, we can consider the negation, which in a way constitutes the entire essence of *nothing*, as bearing on the preposition *ex* itself: God has made the world *of* nothing, that is to say, *not of* anything. This is indeed so because at the origin there was nothing either inside or outside God which could serve as material for the creation of the world. Simply put, there is in God the *total Possibility* of all creatable beings, which must not be understood as a passive possibility or potentiality (there is nothing potential in God), but as an *active* possibility not distinguished from the divine Essence itself. We shall have to return to this cardinal point in the course of the following chapters. From this derive two equally fundamental consequences for our purpose.

First, to say that at the origin there was nothing except God is to say that creation is not a change, since all change presupposes something *which* changes, that is, a subject which as such is equally present at the point of departure and at the point of arrival. Here there is nothing at the point of departure, nor is there really even any point of departure. But if creation is not a change, what is it? It is this: *considered in the creature, creation is not other than its relation to God the Creator*, who is the total and unique Principle of its being. With his habitual calm St Thomas states that, understood passively, creation is in the creature and it is creature. He does not go so far as to say that creation is identical to the creature; he restricts himself to saying that it is creature, adding immediately that this does not make it necessary to seek another principle for it

21. *Summa Theologica*, IaP, Qs 45, 46.

because, being pure relation, it is entirely *ad aliquid*, which is to say that in some way it has its center outside itself, in Another in whom it is as if suspended. As example he gives the Trinitarian relations. Every real *created* relation is still an accident and therefore *of* substance. Indeed, we should recall that in Scholastic terminology, 'accidental' is in no way synonymous with 'extrinsic', as it has become for moderns. But obviously creation cannot be considered a *part* of the creature. It must therefore be *the* creature envisaged completely under a certain aspect. However, since the *Aliquid*, this 'Other' to whom the creature is referred and in whom it is suspended, is here its *total* and *unique* principle (by definition, since it is a question of creation *ex nihilo*), this aspect is itself necessarily and absolutely first and total, and, to return to the terms used by Nicolas of Cusa, *the creature does not possess any other being proper to it than that of this dependence.* The relation of creation is non-reciprocal, that is to say that it is real only from the side of the creature. The *Divine Essence is not itself relative to anything*, for in God there is relationship only *ad intra*, and these are the Trinitarian relationships.

The second consequence is that, since every *active* possibility is in God, there is no more *being* if creation is included than if it is excluded. The creature is distinct from God and, at the same time, the created *esse* adds nothing to the uncreated *esse*. Simply put, things *are* gratuitously, so to speak; in appearance they are totally self-contained, exterior to the Creator, and yet by their entire being they are *from* and *to* the Creator.

To this point we have considered the idea of creation in general. Philosophically at least, the question must be asked whether the world had a beginning, or if it is created *ab aeterno*, and that such a question arises is equally important for our purpose. To some, the idea of a creation *ab aeterno* appears unintelligible and contradictory. Is this not an indication that the very notion of creation in general is not really understood? It seems to us that this lack of understanding offers at least a partial explanation of the current opinion alluded to in the beginning of the paragraph. Fr Marechal has quite justifiably written, 'Is not the necessity of creation, the reciprocal relationship between God and the world, the most characteristic trait of pantheism?'[22] But does it not constrain God in some way to deny that He might have the possibility of creating *ab aeterno*? Now God is not under any necessity either in fact or in the circumstances of creation so to speak. Sovereignly free and independent, if He created it is not by any requirement, whether conceived as exterior or interior. We must be very careful when we say, for example, that love *moved* God to create beings. In God, Love is not a passion to which He is subject; it is His very Essence,[23] that is to say, pure Act, Sovereignly gratuitous Gift, total Liberty that is incapable of being lost.[24]

Basically, the narrowness of our views concerning creation derives from the fact that we unconsciously apply our imagination to it, and imagination is a faculty essentially ordered to the spatio-temporal domain. We say *nothing* existed, and saying this, we represent *something* to ourselves, a space empty of bodies, a time in which nothing happened. St Thomas sweeps away all these phantasms with a word. Time and creation are created together. 'Before' creation there was nothing, not time, not place, not space, not emptiness; *materia prima* itself, as pure potentiality, is only a sort of ideal limit, we might almost say a necessary conventional representation, and in any case it should be termed 'co-created'; thus it, too, is not 'before' creation. The very expression 'creation in time' cannot but be ambiguous. Creation is not in time, but time is in creation. If we now recall that creation is not a change, we will agree that it is perfectly useless to try to form any representation of it whatsoever. Like God, creation is at once both intelligible (which is not to say comprehensible) and unrepresentable.

We should now consider whether or not the Hindu concept of cosmic illusion as expounded above using the symbol of reflection, offers some analogy with the concept of creation. We have said that both concepts have the same reach, that is to say that everything

22. Joseph Maréchal, *Études sur la Psychologie des Mystiques*, vol. 2, p 85.

23. Cf. 1 John 4:18.

24. A stranger to necessity, God is no less a stranger to contingency. But does it not introduce contingency into God to say that He should not have created? Fundamentally, creation in God remains a *mystery*.

which for the Christian is created, is for the non-dualist illusory. Here 'everything' must be understood to mean the world (or worlds), including 'intelligent beings', that is, to use Western terminology, the entirety of spiritual and material beings. Conversely, what is not illusory for the non-dualist is uncreated for the Christian. There is no third term. We will see, however, that the parallel is not perfectly rigorous because in Hinduism, God-the-Producer himself (*Brahmā*) has an illusory character; the created appearance of creatures being illusory, the creative appearance (or the 'face' of God as Creator) is no less so. There is nothing that is not illusory save the Supreme Self (*Paramātmā*) identified with the Absolute (*Parabrahma*). Conforming to received usage, we provisionally accept the term Absolute, the use of which nevertheless presents some serious drawbacks which we will explain further on.

Let us say it again: *the Self (Ātmā) is not the human soul (jivātmā).* Typical in this regard are the Vedantic hymns of Shankara with their incessant refrain 'I am not', where the word 'I' designates the Self and where all creation is passed in review and rejected in a manner reminiscent of St John of the Cross:

> I am not mind nor intellect, nor thought nor self-consciousness.
> I am not hearing nor taste nor smell nor sight,
> I am not ether[25] nor earth nor fire nor air,
> I am pure Intelligence and Bliss,
> I am Shiva, I am Shiva.

> I am not the vital breath nor the five winds
> I am not the seven components of the body nor the five sheaths.
> I am not the five organs of action.
> I am pure Intelligence and Bliss.
> I am Shiva, I am Shiva.

> I have no aversion, no attraction, no avidity, no deviation.
> I feel neither pride nor envy.
> I have no obligations, no interests, no desires; I hope for no

---

25. In this verse it is obviously a question of the five *bhūtas* or corporeal elements; this is why we read 'ether' rather than 'space'.

liberation.
I am pure Intelligence and Bliss.
I am Shiva, I am Shiva.

For me there are neither good acts nor impurities, neither pleasure nor suffering.
Likewise there exist no ritual incantations, holy places, the Vedas or sacrificial act.
I am neither pleasure nor that which can be enjoyed nor the agent of pleasure.
I am pure Intelligence and Bliss.
I am Shiva, I am Shiva.

I know neither death nor doubt nor distinction of caste.
Nor father nor mother. I have never been born.
I have no friend, no relative, no master, no disciple.
I am pure Intelligence and Bliss.
I am Shiva, I am Shiva.

I am without determinant, without form.
By my ubiquity, I am not unrelated to all the sense organs.
I know neither liberation nor servitude.
I am pure Intelligence and Bliss.
I am Shiva, I am Shiva.[26]

We said above that the inability to conceive the possibility of a creation *ab aeterno* suggested that the idea of creation in general was not truly understood. Adopting the point of view of *Advaita*, we would like to raise a kind of symmetrical difficulty, and speak of the idea of a creation *in aeternum*. All intelligent beings (at least) are destined to a life without end—'Siempre, siempre!' [Always, always] the great Teresa repeated in ecstasy. Certainly there is no question of necessity on the part of God, who at each instant remains sovereignly free to annihilate or, if preferred, to 'uncreate', although we are assured that such an eventuality is excluded, God being what He is. From this rises the following difficulty, which might be raised by

---

26. Shankara, *Six Stances sur le Nirvanâ* (*Nirvanashatkam*), cited in Paul Martin-Dubost, *Çankara et le Vedānta* (Paris: Seuil, 1973), p27.

a non-dualist: 'So according to you the divine *esse* and the created *esse* subsist, *eternally juxtaposed*. Are we not right in saying that it is useless for you to claim to have gone beyond dualism?' This is exactly the position of Shankara: 'If the universe, such as we see it, were real, the element of non-dualism would never cease to exist.'[27] There is only one possible response: to show, as we have done, that considered from the perspective of the creature, creation is nothing but its relation to God as to its unique and total principle, and that thus understood, this relationship is the totality of the creature, *any other principle being excluded by hypothesis* (creation *ex nihilo*). This actual, non-temporal creation-relation, literally 'existentiating' the relationship and establishing it in being, makes of the creature a reflection which is entirely constituted by the radiation of the divine Sun. In passing, we note that we can make use of these views for an exegesis of the famous vision of St Benedict, so unusual in the West, and recounted by St Gregory as follows.

[W]hile the disciples were still asleep, Benedict, the man of the Lord, was already awake anticipating the hour of night prayer. He was standing before his window praying to the All-powerful Lord when suddenly, at that hour of the night, he saw a flash of light which chased away the darkness and showed with such splendor that its brightness would have dimmed the brightness of day. While he looked at it, something extraordinary happened; as he later recounted it, *the entire world shrank into itself before his eyes, like a single ray of the sun.*[28]

Thus the harmony between the Western notion of creation and the Hindu idea of cosmic illusion (or divine manifestation) is rendered manifest. We do not claim that they are identical; we say only that they are in no way irreconcilable, as might be believed at first sight.

---

27. Shankara, *Le plus beau fleuron de la discrimination*, trans. by Marcel Sauton (Paris: Adrien Maisonneuve, 1946, v.232), or *Vivekachudamani*, hereafter cited as *VCM*. [The numbering differs in the various English translations we have consulted, and none agrees with the numbering offered here. We give the citation exactly as the author has it. TRS]

28. Gregory I, Pope, *Vita sancti Benedicti*, chap. xxxv (J.-P. Migne, *Patrologia Latina*, vol 66, col. 198).

But perhaps it will be objected that to make of the creature a pure reflection in this way is to reduce it to an appearance without substance, to 'desubstantialize' it, as it were. It is therefore important to understand that what is here involved is not a *direct* comparison of the creature to a reflection, but rather an analogy of proportionality. In other words, in no way do we claim that the creature *is* a reflection. What we say is precisely this: what the reflection is to the object, the creature, *the real and subsistent creature*, is to God. It is thus not to reduce the creature to pure appearance; far from it. It is, on the contrary, to base it in truth. If the creature were not the reflection of *Being*, then it *would not be*.

Let us be permitted a question. Does not the difficulty which some experience in accepting these views arise at least in part from a confusion that is not necessarily conceptual, but vital, between *substantiality* and *aseity*? In any case, it is definitely such a confusion that is clearly revealed in the following lines of Karl Marx:

> It has become practically impossible to ask if there exists an unknown being, a being set above nature and man, this question implying the non-essentiality of nature and of man.[29]

We should thus recall that aseity consists in owing existence only to oneself (*a se*). We shall have to return to this notion at greater length, for it is fundamental for *Advaita*. But it may also be asked if the confusion between aseity and substantiality, to some degree knowingly cultivated in accordance with what we wrote above concerning the attitude of the 'world', does not in its turn betray a kind of claim against God for the ownership of our being. This might well be symbolized by the behavior of the Prodigal Son leaving the paternal home after having demanded *his own part* of the undivided Good of the Father, while his brother, who, according to this interpretation, is not other than the Prodigal himself, receives this response from the Father: 'Son, thou art always with Me, and all I have is thine.'[30]

---

29. Karl Marx, *Le Capital*, vol. VI, Œuvres complètes de Karl Marx, trans. Joseph Roy, J. Molitor (Paris: Alfred Costes), p40.
30. Luke 15:31; cf. John 17:10: 'And all my things are thine, and thine are mine.'

After examining the concept of creation—and we believe no one will doubt its importance for the issue that here occupies us—let us return to the Hindu doctrine of non-dualism (*advaita-vada*). It is absolutely indispensable to keep the following in mind if we wish to avoid pantheism: if everything is relative to the Self, *the Self itself is not relative to anything*. In particular, it is necessary to avoid seeing the Self as a subject of attribution. In this regard the doctrine has a clarity that leaves nothing wanting. All that is imputed to the Self is so imputed by 'worldly' illusion, and it is precisely this 'false imputation' or 'superimposition' (*adhyasa*), of which the classic example is that of the man taking a rope for a serpent, which we will study below. This false imputation gives birth to the chain of existences (*samsara*). In theological language it would be said that in the relation uniting God with all creatures, on the one hand, and, on the other, all creatures to God, only the relation of creatures to God is real, which amounts to saying that from the divine perspective creatures do not exist *as external*. It would therefore be gravely erroneous to conceive the Self as a 'person' in the philosophical sense of *suppositum*. We shall return to this, too, for it is fundamental. The Self is 'from itself' (*a se*, which is aseity), alone in its all-embracing infinity, anterior to all multiplicity and even to Unity, free from all conditioning and from all determination, without parts, as we shall see further on, nor is there anything truly outside It. It is not a nature, it is without quiddity, without qualities; it is actionless, because 'he who acts is other'. All these points will be developed further on. We can see the ambiguity of the common assertion that in the Vedānta the essence of the soul is identical to *Brahma*. If the word 'soul' is understood in the generally received philosophical and theological sense of the West, this is an error. Moreover, we shall have to further specify these questions of terminology, a common source of much confusion. Only *Brahma* is identical to *Brahma* without it even being possible to say that this identity is *real*, there where all dualism has ceased even to the very unity of pure Being, principle of universal Existence. The Absolute is not relative to anything. It is a tautology. It is therefore without real relation to the essence of the soul in the precise philosophical sense of this term, that is to say, in the sense in which the being of the soul as determined and delimited by its essence, does, by this fact, admit of definition.

And here let us rule out a possible interpretation of our thinking. It might be thought that since each creature has its proper essence which limits the existence received from God, we avoid the danger of pantheism while emphasizing the identity of God's existence and our own. For our part, we certainly would not speak of identity between God's existence and our own, for such a manner of speaking suggests that between God's *esse* and ours there is a univocality which, so to speak, is the extreme opposite of our view. On the contrary, we are persuaded that between the one and the other, the analogy verges on the equivocality of an infinitesimal 'quantity' without being reduced thereto, which *ipso facto* would reduce the created being to nothing; and this is translated as perfectly as possible by the image of the reflection 'without reality'. *Quis ut Deus?* God alone is identical with God; or if a different manner of expression is preferred, *God is identity.*

This may seem a digression, but since the occasion presents itself, let us say concerning this last formula inspired by our Trinitarian faith, how much we deplore reading from a Catholic source that God is 'triple'. This is much more than a simple question of words. 'Quae non triplex sed trinitas et dici et credi debet' (That one must say and believe not triple, but Trinity), states the Council of Toledo (AD 675). God is simple, absolutely and without reserve. In fact, on the one hand God *is* the divinity, and, on the other, the divinity is not divided between three divine Persons but pertains equally to all and to each in his indivisible totality. More precisely still, since each divine Person, although really distinct from each of the others, is not really distinct from the divinity, each *is* the divinity. We see no contradiction between non-dualism and Trinity. Moreover, we do not believe that any other conception of the 'Supreme Reality' would have any chance of acceptance by a non-dualist, no more by a Muslim than by a Jew. The demand of unity requires of the Christian the greatest precision in the formulation of his faith. Later on we will return to the relation that can be established between non-dualism and Trinity; for now let us again cite Nicolas of Cusa:

In God, the Trinity is not composed, it is neither plural nor numerical. It is absolutely simple. . . . And if simpler terms [than those of Father, Son, and Spirit] could be found, they would be better suited, for example, Unity, Quiddity, and Identity.[31]

Thus God, and God alone, *is* identity. All that which, *sensu composito*, identifies God and created existence is pantheism (see below for the way in which *sensu composito* is to be understood in this context). The Vedantic doctrine of non-dualism embraces an uneasy antinomy, but one that it is essential to grasp and which merits all the concentration of our intelligence.

One does not *become Brahma*, so if the Delivered is really identical to *Brahma*, this can mean only one thing, that 'the Delivered' is a Name of *Brahma*. We will try to clarify this eminently paradoxical assertion by making use of the distinction well known in traditional logic of a proposition that can be understood either in a 'composite sense' (*sensu composito*), or in a 'divided sense' (*sensu diviso*). We are familiar with the classic example, the blind man sees. It is a contradiction in the 'composite sense', but it is possible in the 'divided sense', that is, once the blindness has been removed or 'separated' from the subject who was blind. Analogically, our case is the same. If we say that the man or the world is *Brahma*, understanding this *sensu composito*, we utter a contradiction (and in addition, a blasphemy). But if we understand it *sensu diviso*, that is to say, if we understand that man *is not* man or that the world *is not* the world, that *I am not who I am*, then it becomes possible and no longer implies a contradiction. We will try to translate into terms of Western logic what Hindu logic expresses by means of the notion of 'implicit meaning' (*lakshana*).[32] What this signifies precisely will appear more clearly when we study the symbol of the rope that a man perceives as a serpent.

However, it is important to understand the singularity (in the etymological sense) of the 'division' between man as subject and man as attribute, *a division which is not the effect of a change realized*

---

31. Nicolas of Cusa, *Œuvres choisies*, pp 432–433 [specific work not given TRS].
32. Cf *VCM*, vv. 247–249.

in becoming, as in the example of a blind man, but which is constitutive of contingent existence as such. Thus, *sensu divisus* in a sense
that is not precisely identical to that which it has in Western logic,
but its analogical transposition; real *sensus divisus,* nevertheless,
removing the logical contradiction (man is not man) because it signifies that here the verb 'to be' does not have the sense of a pure
grammatical copula, but rather expresses (or suggests insofar as
possible), the antinomy that is constitutive of contingent existence.
We see that here we are at the antipodes of philosophical pantheism,
and probably nowhere else are the absolute transcendence and the
marvelously intimate immanence of the divine Reality both asserted
with such energy. For us this recalls what Fr Tilliette wrote of Cardinal Daniélou in the review *Axes*:

> He already fully acknowledges the absolute transcendence of
> God who, for this very reason, is excluded from all alterity—the
> Wholly Other is the Not-Other (Nicolas of Cusa)—and is there-
> fore the Emmanuel who has pitched his tent among us.[33]

It may be of some interest to note in this connection that in Hebrew
the two divine names *El-Elion* (Most-High God) and *Emmanuel*
(God with us) have the same number, obtained by the addition of
the numerical values of the letters composing them, unexpectedly
underlining the coincidence *in re* of the divine Transcendence and
Immanence.[34]

Since the above exposition obviously constitutes the kernel of our
argument, we must pause here a little longer, because it could now
be argued that notwithstanding all our explanations, a contradictory proposition is a contradictory proposition, and if we recognize
the validity of the principle of non-contradiction—which in fact we
do—our exposition is without value. We thus say the following: in
order that the proposition 'man is not man' be something other
than a simple contradiction, it is necessary and sufficient that 'man'

---

33. *Axes,* vol. VII, 1974/5, p93.
34. The number of each of these names is 197. It seems that René Guénon was
the first to call attention to their numerical equivalence; cf. *Le Roi du Monde* (Paris:
Gallimard, 1976), p50.

(subject) and 'man' (predicate) not be considered in the same respect. Now this is in fact the case. In the first instance, the subject as such is considered; in the second, the predicate as such. In other words, the first designates the man *who* is; the second, the man *that* he is. Someone may insist that there is a unity, an identity between the one and the other! We answer that there is a certain unity, a certain identity; in other words, a unity, an identity that are not absolute but relative, for there are degrees of unity and there are degrees of identity. If this were not so, such expressions as Supreme Unity (applied to the Unity of the Trinity) or that of 'Supreme Identity' (in Hinduism and Sufism) would be devoid of meaning, while in fact they do have meaning, meaning that is of prime importance for the understanding of being (since *unam* and *ens convertuntur*).

We have just alluded to a distinction between the man *who* is and the man *that* he is. This may call to mind the Thomist doctrine concerning the distinction in every contingent being between essence and existence. In fact this is one of the possible senses of the proposition under consideration, which would then mean that man (existence) is not man (essence). It is quite obvious that here we have no contradiction. Nevertheless, even if an analogy exists with the non-dualist concept, it would be wrong simply to equate the two points of view. Furthermore, if the equation were justified, we would not have avoided pantheism, since not only is the Creator-creature distinction essential in the philosophical sense stated above, it is also fully existential. However, we cannot rule out the possibility that an in-depth study of the Hindu doctrine of non-dualism might shed additional light on the distinction between essence and existence, matter and form, or act and potency.

We will try to clarify the point of view of this doctrine more fully and in a more positive manner, an undertaking that will last throughout the chapters that follow, since the present chapter is only an introduction. As we wrote, every creature has its own essence which, in a way, circumscribes and determines for it the existence received from God. The *esse* of the creature thus appears as a certain determination or delimitation of the divine *esse* which, however, in Itself remains rigorously undetermined and undeterminable in Its infinity, eternally distinct from the created *esse*. It is this *esse* in itself, and not the created *esse*, which is real being according to the Hindu perspective. (Of course, we only use the notion 'created' in order to make ourself better understood, for it is alien to Hinduism.) This real being, which is in no way a property of the creature, and which cannot belong to it nor be attributed to it in any capacity or in any manner in which one might wish to understand the matter, is nevertheless true uncreated being *to which*, as we wrote in our exegesis of St Bernard, the entire creature belongs, and *from which* it entirely, immediately, and presently depends in all that it is. And in order to avoid any pantheistic misunderstanding, let us once again recall that according to Advaita, this being in and of itself has no real relation whatsoever to anything outside of itself, and that it is not a 'person' (in the sense of suppositum).

The *advaitin* who seeks 'realization' methodically situates himself at the 'point of view' of this being in virtue of the sacred formula *Aham Brahmāsmi*, 'I am *Brahma*', which we shall analyze in the next chapter, or some other analogous formula properly received from his guru. If we expressed this reversal of viewpoint in Biblical terms, we would say that the *advaitin* has passed from the perspective defined by the divine Name YHWH (He-Is) to that defined by the divine Name *Ehyeh* (I-Am).[35] It goes without saying that here on the 'razor's edge', incessantly exposed to a properly Luciferian vertigo, this peril alone would suffice to justify the necessity commonly maintained in India, for whoever is engaged on this path to place himself under a spiritual Master and to obey him in all things. But even if he actually skirts vertiginous abysses, if he is constantly threatened with the worst spiritual catastrophes, we must remember that in itself the doctrine of non-dualism is intellectually and spiritually at the antipodes of pantheism, just as, whatever the outward appearance, it also excludes all 'polytheism' and every formal idolatry; and it is this that in our eyes makes it of interest as the foundation of a possible doctrinal accord with the Catholic Church. It seems that the Abbot Monanchin held a position very close to our own in this regard. Envisaging a possible 'Christian metamorphosis of yoga', he in fact wrote, 'I am inclined to believe

---

35. Cf Exodus 3:14: 'I-Am hath sent me unto you.'

that if this metamorphosis should come to pass, it will be accomplished through the Vedānta, but 'I am not a prophet nor of the school of the prophets.'[36]

To end this chapter, in which we have taken a rather 'harmonizing' approach, one question remains to be asked. If Deliverance as set forth by the Vedānta consists essentially in placing oneself 'in the place and position' of God, if one may so speak, does this not thereby imply a divine and supernatural intervention? 'He whom the Self has chosen, he alone can attain Him', declares the *Katha Upanishad.* Should we not therefore hold that the Vedantic teaching on this point has its source in a true 'revelation' and that its realization, or rather its verification, in man postulates divine grace in the precise theological sense of this word? We cannot claim to answer these questions in a fully satisfactory manner, nor do we have the authority to do so. All that we can assert is that these questions must in fact be considered. Perhaps we can formulate them in another way. Has Hinduism had its prophets, understanding this word in the etymological sense of God's mouthpiece? If we refer to the statements of Pope Paul VI at the general audience of December 9, 1964, on his return from Bombay, there appears to be no doubt of the response.

> St Augustine, though stern in maintaining the necessary relationship between the Church and salvation, wrote, 'It should not be doubted that the Gentiles, too, have their prophets' (*Contra Faustus,* 19, 2; *PL* 42, col. 348). We have had this impression of values worthy of honor as we have approached the great Indian people. This impression is not settled in irenicism or syncretism, but it imposes on the apostolic dialogue much moderation, wisdom, and patience.[37] These words call for meditation. We should

---

36. *Axes,* vol. VIII, article on the problems of Christian yoga, n17.
37. *Documentation Catholique,* 1439, January 3, 1965.

not, however, neglect to consider with equal seriousness the question which Cardinal Marella asked himself during a lecture given at the Pontifical Urban University. 'When even among Catholic authors . . . it is proclaimed that the various religions of the earth are "normal ways of salvation", depositaries of an analogous if not identical divine revelation, . . we wonder if in the wake of the Council we can still believe that we are line with the Christian tradition, that we are faithful to the deposit transmitted by the Apostles to the Church?'[38]

Whatever one's thoughts on this point, it is in any case clear that for the Christian a divine intervention of this kind, whatever the mode, cannot but be ordered to the mystery of the God-Man and His sacrifice, unique principle of reconciliation and salvation. As for the effective realization in man of this theoretical Vedantic teaching, its possibility cannot be separated from at least an implicit faith in the divine Word *made man*. By virtue of this faith, and this faith alone (obviously what is involved is a faith informed by charity), I can in truth say, 'It is no longer I who live,' or, in other terms, it is no longer I who exist (since, according to St Thomas, for someone alive, to live is to exist), it is Christ who exists in me, or, better still, in me it is Christ who exists. This interpretation is supported by the testimony of two pontifical teachings. Treating of Christian identity at the general audience of July 18, 1973, Pope Paul VI spoke of the 'Eucharistic action . . . where operating in Christ himself, we translate in sacramental language the *fullness of our supernatural identity*: "I live, yet not I, but Christ liveth in me."'[39] More recently, in his encyclical *Redemptor hominis* of March 4, 1979, John Paul II stated:

The man who wishes to understand himself thoroughly—and not just in accordance with immediate, partial, often superficial, and even illusory standards and measures of his being—he must with his unrest, uncertainty, even his weakness and sinfulness, with his life and death, draw near to Christ. He must, so to

---

38. Conference on the Propogation of the Faith held at the Pontifical Urban University, November 21, 1968; cf. *Documentation Catholique*, 1532, January 19, 1969.
39. *Documentation Catholique*, August 5–19 1973, p704.

speak, enter into him with all his own self, he must 'appropriate' and assimilate the whole of the reality of the Incarnation and Redemption in order to find himself.[40]

We have spoken of the necessity of at least an implicit faith in the divine Word made man; but can faith in a guru identified with the divine Word (*shabda-brahma*) and venerated as his human aspect, be considered an implicit faith in the Word made man? We shall have occasion below to cite a verse of Shankara's *Vivekacudamani* which admits of such an interpretation. In virtue of faith in Christ, true God and true man, a new *being* is given to me like a new superpersonal, supernatural, and superessential subject, who is not multiple, and who is to the individual that I am 'according to the flesh', what this latter is to all that can be imputed to it, attributes, qualities, operations—in short, who is to me a new intimate superpersonal principle of *existence*. It can be seen that the terminology of Dionysius comes spontaneously to the pen as soon as we try to express non-dualist concepts in terms of Western philosophy. We deliberately write '*like* a new subject', reserving treatment of the *singularity* of the hypostatic union for following chapters. As of now, however, we can note that it is difficult to situate the singular case of the Man-God in the doctrinal framework of non-dualism as we have expounded it. It would be appropriate to examine how from an Indian point of view the particular case of *Avatāras* or 'divine descents' are situated in relation to the general assertion of the *actual* identity of the Self and of *Brahma*. The doctrine of the Avataras is developed particularly in the Vishnuite tradition.

It seems to us that such might be a Christian expression of the divine Word envisaged as the universal Self, an expression which, we believe, would betray neither the transcendence of the divine Revelation in Jesus Christ nor the spirit of the *Upanishads*. May they become *One*! We hasten to add, however, that we do not nourish too great illusions as to the early chances of such a reconciliation. When

---

40. *Redemptor hominis*, no. 10, AAs 71 (1979), p274. This passage is repeated in the same words in the Apostolic Exhortation *Catechesi tradendae* of October 16, 1979, n61.

we ask God for the unity of Christians, then the unity of believers, and finally for the unity of all men, the Lord has no other response for us than that which he gave the mother of the sons of Zebedee, 'You know not what you ask. Can you drink the chalice that I shall drink?'[41]

Because of the point of view adopted in this first chapter, we have at this stage only arrived at an indirect and rather external vision of non-dualism, one that might be provided by a Christian or, if preferred, a 'Christianizing' interpretation. Such a view, even if not necessarily partial, is nevertheless very incomplete ('one-sided', as is said in English), and it would be quite illusory to be content with it. When we envisage a Christian 'non-dualism', we have in view something much larger. Our undertaking has therefore only just begun. What we have said until now should be viewed as an approach particularly adapted to the Western and Christian mentality. We believe this approach to be legitimate from the Hindu point of view, but it is only an approach. It remains for us to consider the doctrine in itself and for itself, *from inside*, according to an expression used by Cardinal Koenig in one of his interventions in the Second Vatican Council. This is what we shall attempt to do beginning with the following chapter. It is only when our examination is complete and we have acquired a view of the whole that is as exact and exhaustive as possible that we can answer the question: is it legitimate to consider the possibility of a Christian non-dualism?

41. Matt. 20:22.

2

'I AM *BRAHMA*'

IN THE FIRST CHAPTER we considered the Vedantic doctrine of non-dualism not so much in itself but more as an interpretation, which, while undoubtedly legitimate, was developed in part as a function of its possible insertion into a Christian perspective. In this chapter, on the contrary, we deliberately adopt *the standpoint of the doctrine itself.* This will entail the inevitable consequence of making Christianity appear *subordinate,* but it will thereby only better measure how deeply the difficulties of dialogue are rooted.

We are not of the East, nor are we qualified to offer ourself as a representative thereof. We believe, however, that on the whole the following account remains substantially faithful to its spirit and adequately reflects its intellectual and spiritual position, two things which appear closely related if not in fact synonymous as regards non-dualist doctrine. Perhaps this account will also better enable some to grasp more clearly the profound reasons for its intransigence and its 'inconvertibility'.

The title we have given this chapter, 'I am *Brahma*', *Aham Brahmāsmi*, is the central assertion of the Vedantic doctrine of the 'Supreme Identity', which it expresses with an authority equal to, say, the *Shahada*, the *credo* of Islam, 'There is no divinity if it is not the Divinity.' Here, however, it is a question of a wholly interior authority, in principle resting on nothing 'institutional'. It is thus necessary to call attention at the outset to a point of the greatest intellectual and spiritual importance, which is that he who legitimately makes this sentence *his own* is never an unauthorized individual, but someone who has received it from the mouth of a spiritual Master authorized by a *traditio* that is considered efficacious, with an efficacy which, in the last resort, goes all the way back to *Brahma* Itself, for, as we have already noted, 'He whom the Self elects, he alone can attain It.' This is the idea of the 'efficacious word', which the notion of mantra[1] expresses. But let it be said that nothing here permits us to speak of 'magic' as is sometimes done in this case, as also in the case of Islamic *dhikr*, which is comparable in this regard. Indeed, some people would like to characterize the Christian sacraments themselves as 'magic'.

However little one may reflect on the point above, it must at least suggest that for the *advaitin* what is involved is not, as is commonly thought in the West, simply an 'entering into one's own heart' or a return to one's *natural* center, but that this entering in, this return, is regarded in some way as the 'sacrament' of something else. It goes without saying that if we use the term 'sacrament', it is in a purely analogical and 'indicative' manner. But in this connection we would say that for the Christian who tries to enter into the spirit of the Hindu perspective, it can be very enlightening in certain respects—*despite a radical disparity* which we shall have to revisit—to compare the sentence which concerns us, 'I am *Brahma*', with the formula of the Eucharistic consecration, 'This is my Body', the valid pronunciation of which requires a special 'ordination' whose principal effect is to permit the priest to function *in persona Christi*. Moreover, we ask that if Christ were not present in the consecratory prayer, how could he really be present in the consecrated species? And here let us recall the statements of Pope Paul VI cited at the end of the first chapter concerning the Eucharistic action wherein the plenitude of our supernatural identity is translated into sacramental language, *operating in Christ himself*. Among the factors of the just mentioned disparity, let it suffice here to mention only one, that while the consecration effects a *change*, the Supreme Identity, according to non-dualist doctrine, is not the production of a non-preexisting result (Shankara).

---

1. Concerning the doctrine of the mantra, see Arthur Avalon, *La Doctrine du mantra*, Paris: Editions Orientales, 1979, and Giuseppe Tucci, *Théorie et pratique du mandala* (Paris: Fayard, 1974).

I am *Brahma. Aham Brahmāsmi.* Let us now undertake an analysis of our formula, and let us immediately say that it is not simply a question of a logical or grammatical analysis, but of a *real* analysis, by which we mean an analysis which, through a text and words, aims directly at *things.* What interests us is not the logical or grammatical subject, but the real ontological subject, the *being* who says 'I'. It is important to recall what we wrote in the first chapter: only God is identical to God. Everything that identifies God and created existence *sensu composito,* in the composite sense, is pantheism. Vedantic doctrine embraces an antinomy which is difficult to grasp, but essential; further, the *advaitin* who seeks 'realization' situates himself methodically at the 'point of view' of this *being* (real or divine) by means of the sacred formula, *Aham Brahmāsmi,* I am *Brahma.*

Aham Brahmāsmi, I am *Brahma.* What does this say? There are two possibilities. Either the speaker is one 'delivered in this life', or he is not. If the latter, the assertion as it relates to the individual who enunciates it, is the expression of a 'not real' knowledge, that is, a knowledge of a speculative or purely theoretical character, which is not yet 'realized' for the man in question even though *That* which expresses this 'unreal' knowledge remains always supremely real in Itself. Thus, in its obvious sense, insofar as the speaker 'exists', the declaration 'I am *Brahma*' expresses an 'objective confusion' which is properly pantheistic. This I in question is not *Brahma* but a 'produced being' (we would say a creature). At least this would be so if there were not three things to be considered.

The first is that by hypothesis (since we are speaking of a non-dualist), the human speaker himself knows theoretically that as such this manifested 'I' is illusory, and therefore as such is not *Brahma* any more than it is the veritable Self. Basically we can say that there is coincidence between 'manifested', 'created', and 'illusory'. The created being is the being of illusion, the reflection of which the Truth is the non-manifested. The manifested being is illusory as such, that is, precisely insofar as it appears as something other than *Brahma,* as we shall see below when we speak of the man who takes a rope for a serpent. We specify further that the 'manifested' should be understood as everything that can be known, *within* as well as without.

The second thing to consider is that, as we have said, the speaker adopts this formula in a 'methodological' manner, that is to say that he uses it as a support for meditation or of realization, even, if you will, as an 'invocation', as a prayer, since there are incontestably two distinct realities here, two 'persons' in the Western psychological sense. On the one hand there is a human individual, as such illusory in the sense discussed, but real on the cosmological plane under consideration, that of empirical existence; on the other, confronting him, is *Brahma*, or more precisely (since distinction and dualism remain, and *Brahma* has no counterpart), a 'principial manifestation' of *Brahma*, which is not *Brahma* in itself, or the supreme *Brahma* (*Parabrahma*), but *Brahmā* or the Non-supreme (*Aparabrahma*), producer of beings *and himself 'illusory' with regard to the Supreme*, of which he is as it were the 'face' or the appearance. Let the reader note that we write *Brahma* (without the macron) for the infinite *Brahma*, and *Brahmā* (with the macron) for the Producer of beings. We will return to this distinction, which is of primary importance.[2]

Finally, the third thing to consider is that, as already noted at the beginning of the chapter, the speaker is not an individual lacking a mandate, but the *vehicle* of a *traditio* which, of 'non-human' (*apaurushēya*) origin, authorizes this practice in a quasi-sacramental way.

We have just analyzed the case of the speaker who has not yet realized for himself the 'Supreme Identity'. Note that we say 'for himself', for even if not realized in this sense, the Supreme Identity *is* the

---

2. There is an essential and fundamental distinction between *Brahma* and *Brahmā*. In brief it is that which Eckhart makes between *Godhead* and *God*, or which Palamite theology marks with its distinction between the *Divine Essence* and the *Divine Energies*. *Brahma* is the Supreme Principle and *Brahmā* the creative agent and personal God. Some awareness of this is necessary for readers because the concepts are critical to understanding the author's remarks. The distinction is either explicit or implicit throughout this work, and this is so for two reasons: because Hindus, notwithstanding their numerous personifications of the Divine, constantly have *Brahma* in mind as ultimate referent, whereas Christian conceptions generally stop at the ontological level, that of God as Person, which is that of *Brahmā* (spelled with a macron over the final *a*). The convention in English is to use the term *Brahman* for the supreme, and *Brahma* for the non-supreme; we have retained the orthography of the French transliteration. TRS

Reality, *whether or not the being is delivered.* Fundamentally, this is the ultimate justification for one who is not yet delivered to use the formula of the Supreme Identity. And this leads to an examination of the case of the speaker who is 'delivered in life' (*jivan-mukta*).

Aham Brahmāsmi, I am *Brahma*. Who is this 'I' in the case of the speaker 'delivered in life'? It is the true Self (*Ātmā*), since *Ātmā* is *Brahma*. But, more precisely, what is the Self? The doctrine of non-dualism does not identify the Self with 'God' (*Ishvara*), *the qualified Brahmā* (*saguna*), Producer of beings, but rather with *Brahma* unqualified (*nirguna*) and supreme (*Parabrahma*), the Infinite which leaves nothing outside Itself, or rather, which has no within or without. This means that the Self is Itself 'non-qualified', free of all determination or limitation, *including this first determination which is that of pure Being, Principle of universal manifestation.*

We have just said that the 'manifested' must be understood to mean all that can be perceived or conceived, whether within or without. The Self as such, as *Brahma*, from which It is in no way distinguished, is absolutely unmanifest and unmanifestable. If in a certain sense the living soul (*jivātmā*) can be regarded as a manifestation of *Ātmā*, it is only in the sense that *Ātmā* is 'that which manifests everything, without being Itself manifested by anything whatsoever'. Neither the higher intellect (*buddhi*), nor the mental (*manas*), nor the sense of self—a Westerner would say the 'human person' (*ahankara*, literally 'that which makes the I', *aham*)—none of these is the Self. Strictly speaking, it should be said that *Ātmā is nothing*, nothing that can be perceived, nothing that can be conceived or known in any manner whatsoever. Like *Brahma*, *Ātmā* is 'Non-Being', which is not to say 'nothingness' (it would be better to avoid this term which, since it is grammatically a substantive, amounts to a 'substantiation' of nothing), but, on the contrary—if 'nothingness' could have a contrary—we would be tempted to say that *Ātmā is what escapes all determination whatsoever, including the first determination which is that of pure Being itself. Ātmā* is beyond all perception, conception, or experience in general, beyond all things implying subject and object; beyond all existence and all essence, even beyond pure Being, as we said, and therefore beyond Unity, with which Being is coextensive; in short, *beyond*

God (*Ishvara* or *Brahmā*). Let us pause at this last point, for in a way, this is where the specificity of the non-dualist Eastern spirit lies, a specificity so difficult for a Westerner to appreciate correctly.

For Dr Jacques Albert Cuttat, the root of the East-West (Christian) contrast lies in the opposition of 'solitary interiority' and 'reciprocal interiority', and he sees the superiority of the 'reciprocal interiority' in a *tremendous heightening of the enstasis when face to face with the absolute 'Thou'.*[3] In our view, this contains a mistake as regards the Orient, for 'interior solitude' (*kaivalya*) is not Deliverance (*moksha*). It is certainly understandable that the tremendous interiority of the Orient, being what is most opposed to our own tendencies, should have so vividly impressed Westerners that they should have been tempted to consider it as the whole of Eastern spirituality. However, the confusion is also, and more profoundly, explained by the absence of any exterior criteria to distinguish the state of the 'Delivered' from that of the 'Solitary', this distinction being properly im-perceptible, in-conceivable, and in-expressible. We have already noted that from an Eastern perspective, a mantra draws its entire efficacy from its 'non-human' origin (*apaurusheya*), which would suggest that it must be something more than a simple 'entry of man into his own heart'. Certainly, if Eastern spirituality were nothing more than simple interiority, it could seem easy to admit the superiority of Christianity. Should not the fact that this is not the case suggest that there is a fundamental error of interpretation?

Hindu thought is familiar with and acknowledges a distinction between God (Ishvara, *Brahmā*) and the soul (*jivātmā*). In one sense this dualism is irreducible, and we can again observe that the *Infinite excludes all distinction*. Within the cosmic illusion, Hindu thought also admits a hierarchy of degrees corresponding to those of 'divine manifestation', which is what permits us to speak of 'Deliverance by

3. Jacques Albert Cuttat, *Expérience chrétienne et spiritualité orientale* (Paris: Desclée de Brouwer, 1967), pp103, 296.

degrees' (*krama-moksha*), even though Deliverance, once realized, is absolutely discontinuous with any conditioned state whatsoever, however elevated. We draw particular attention to the following: we have just spoken of 'degrees of manifestation'. For the non-dualist, to one degree or another all manifestation is illusory as such, *even if it be a question of 'principal manifestation', which corresponds to the degree of Pure Being, that is, in Western terms, to 'God' Himself.* Besides, does not the existence of the 'not-God' rule out 'God' as the Infinite? 'All externally added conditionings (*upādhi*), from *Brahmā* to a blade of grass, are illusory'.[4] However, we must be careful not to say that 'God' is illusory *for man*; quite the contrary, God is the Truth of man, as the object is the truth of the reflection. He is illusory (in the sense of corresponding to a lesser degree of reality) only with regard to the Infinite, because the Latter is truly 'without a second"; and if 'God' is illusory with regard to the Infinite it is because *in reality* He *is* the Infinite, outside of which there is nothing, neither 'God' nor 'not-God'. The Infinite is, so to speak, the common Essence of 'God' (*Brahmā*, the Producer of beings) and of the 'soul' (*jivātmā*), *both considered apart from all that makes them distinct and thus their reciprocal limitation.*[5] There is nothing absolutely real except the unmanifestable unmanifest, that is, 'Non-being' in the sense we have indicated, supreme, unqualified *Brahma* (*Parabrahma*), totally unconditioned and unlimited. It is That which is the true Self present in every being, the Supreme Self (*Paramātmā*). *Aham Brahmāsmi*, I am *Brahma*.

These principles, briefly noted, allow us to understand why Western attempts to persuade the East that a 'reciprocal interiority' (which is a 'reciprocal limitation'), is superior to a 'solitary interiority', are doomed to failure. We said above that the state of the 'Solitary' cannot be considered Deliverance (*moksha*). This is not exact except as this state is understood in the West, where it is seen as nothing more than the perfect 'reintegration' of the 'human person'

---

4. *VCM*, v. 386.

5. 'They are superimpositions applied to *Ishvara* (God) and to the *jiva* (the soul). If you manage to separate them all, you will no longer find either *Ishvara* or *Jiva*.' *VCM*, v. 244.

in its deepest center. In itself, such a degree is *infinitely* removed from Deliverance. Furthermore, it could happen that this state might render Deliverance impossible if it permanently imprison the Solitary in what a Buddhist text calls 'the (illusory) conviction that I am.' In certain respects this is somewhat analogous to the 'spiritual pride' of Western theology. We say 'in certain respects', for, from an Eastern point of view, 'reciprocal interiority' itself (the *noverim me, noverim Te* of St Augustine [that I may know Thee, who knowest me, *Confessions* x.1.1.2]) proceeds from the same ignorance (*avidya*) of the true Self. For the Orient, whether it is a question of 'pride' or 'humility', it is all fundamentally of the same order and is situated on the same level, although it bears very diverse fruit in the domain of the 'individual soul' (*jivātmā*). What follows will permit this to be still better understood.

We said above that the distinction between God (*Ishvara*) and the soul (*jivātmā*) was, in a sense, irreducible. For the non-dualist, as soon as the one and the other are manifested (even if this manifestation is 'eternal', for it is not a question of duration but of nature), they are both *produced together*, face to face, distinct one from the other (recall the image of the sun and its reflection), just as the image in the mirror and the object are produced and withdrawn together, although belonging to very different degrees of reality. But when, according to the beautiful expression of Shankara, 'the Sun of Knowledge arises in the heaven of the heart', then the soul appears illusory, *and simultaneously, so also does God who produced it*. Then all dualism ceases, and even all unity insofar as this latter is coextensive with Pure Being, principle of all manifestation and all multiplicity, and there remains only the immense and incomparable Reality of Non-Being (*Parabrahma*) *that has always been. Aham Brahmāsmi.* I am *Brahma*. This is why the 'withdrawal of God' is regarded in India as a possible indication of Deliverance, and the *lamma sabacthani* of Christ is also frequently interpreted in this way. It can be seen how 'reciprocal interiority' might be judged from this perspective, appearing to Hindu eyes only as an inferior degree on the way to integral Realization, and how the insistence with which Christians proclaim its superiority would confirm their unfavorable opinion of these latter, if not of Christianity itself.

If we had to summarize in a few words the essential position of the non-dualist Orient, we would say that it is God who saves the created 'human person' by rendering him perpetually 'blessed' (here 'perpetually' signifying until the 'night of *Brahma*', that is to say until the return of the manifested universe into the non-manifest), thus *fixing* the being in an 'illusory' state (which caused certain Sufis to say that *Allah* confines the soul in the prison of Paradise), *since, from the perspective of the Supreme, He Himself is 'illusory'*, although Pure Being and the Principle of all manifestation. *It is this definitive fixation of the created 'human person' which properly constitutes salvation.*[6] But because it does not dispel ignorance (*avidya*) of the true Self, but on the contrary definitively confirms—with the reservation indicated above—the 'human person' in 'the (illusory) conviction that I am,' salvation cannot be identified with Deliverance (*moksha*) from which it remains *infinitely* distant. This, even if he does not say so, is what every non-dualist thinks, and this is what it is indispensable to know if one wishes to enter into true dialogue with him.

---

6. Strictly speaking, our anonymous author is correct in limiting the meaning of the term *salvation* as he does. In English usage, however, the fullness of *salvation* can be understood to imply the plenitude of spiritual realization, although we must keep in mind that the common understanding of the term does not envisage passage beyond individuality. TRS

3

'IN ALL THINGS
LIKE UNTO MEN'

AT THE END OF THE FIRST CHAPTER we noted the difficulty of situating the singular case of the Man-God in the framework of non-dualist doctrine as we have expounded it. But must we not go further and say that in this perspective the Man-God no longer appears to be singular, but simply a particular instance, even if borderline, of the common human condition? From this arises the following question, however offensive and incongruous it may appear to Christian eyes. *Is what Catholic theology designates as the 'hypostatic union' not true of every man?* Here we are no longer confronted with an effort, so common in our day, to reduce the 'supernatural' to the 'natural', but on the contrary, with a kind of radical 'supernatural-ization' of all humanity.

We should add that we are perfectly aware how scandalous such a question may appear, even if, as here, it is considered simply as a 'working hypothesis'. Nevertheless, it is a question that has arisen at one time or another for anyone who has tackled the profound thought of India, and we are well aware of the attraction that Indian thought exercises on Western spirituality today. This being so, and since a horrified recoil obviously does not resolve the question, is it not better to accept and confront the problem frankly and without reservation? Moreover, such a hypothesis would in all likelihood move the relevant fields of theology toward a more profound understanding and continued investigation, and thus we think we would be ill advised simply to shrug it aside. Even if we must introduce distinctions and nuances before offering a response; even if, at the end of our research and analysis, nothing remains of the original hypothesis (and we shall see that in reality the identity of the Self and *Brahma* has nothing in common with a *personal* union); even so, throughout our inquiry this hypothesis will have acted like a catalyst which, though not itself entering into the process, nevertheless permits a result impossible to obtain without it.

A host of objections and difficulties immediately arise. Let us examine the most important, which is that since Jesus Christ is the exclusive Son of God, a plurality of *unique* Sons (the plural of *unique* demonstrates this well enough)[1] is a contradiction in terms. To this preliminary and apparently decisive objection, St Thomas has already provided a response which, it seems, has not been accorded the attention it merits. 'Now, the power of a Divine Person is infinite and cannot itself be limited by any created thing. Hence it may not be said that a Divine Person so assumed one human nature as to be unable to assume another.' Here is the Latin text: *Unde non est dicendum quod persona divina ita assumpserit unam naturam humanam quod non potuerit assumere aliam.*[2] The meaning of our hypothesis becomes more precise. We do not wonder if there could be a plurality of 'unique Sons', which, in fact, makes no sense whatsoever, but rather if this Son, eternal and uncreated, may not be the unique personal principle manifesting itself in and through multiple individual human natures, distinct one from another. In sum, our question bears upon the cosmic role of the divine Word, Creator and Redeemer of men, Principle and End of creation, and 'Head' of deified humanity. Having dealt with the preliminary question of the absurdity of our inquiry, we can continue our inquiry.

We are immediately faced with a new difficulty, which, since we are not aware of anything else of its kind, may also appear

---

1. In French, the adjective conforms in number to the noun it modifies, so that here we have what amounts to 'uniques' to modify Sons. TRS

2. *Summa Theologica*, IIIaP, Q 3, a 7.

insurmountable. In order to resolve it, it is necessary that we see very clearly on what level the problem is situated; indeed, we must avoid confusing the ontological and psychological levels, as is so often the tendency today. Furthermore, we could limit ourself to observing that there is no lack of contemporary theologians who hold that Jesus, *in his human psychology,* was not immediately *conscious* (we do not say 'did not know') of his quality as Son, and of his equality with the Father. This is in fact quite tenable, since, with the newborn, human consciousness attains its fullness only progressively with the accumulated perceptions of the various senses. 'Jesus advanced in wisdom, and age, and grace with God and men.'[3] We would like to be permitted a question along this same train of thought. Even without transcending the limits of the merely human order, can we believe that all virtualities included in the 'truth' of man are realized effectively by all men living in these last times of the second millennium of Christianity? But in order to remove all basis for the difficulty confronting us, let it suffice to complete our hypothesis as follows. Is not what theology designates as the hypostatic union true for every man, *even supposing that for a particular man there might be no possibility of effective realization?*

In order to clarify this idea of 'realization', let us recall the explanation of the mantra *Aham Brahmāsmi* from the previous chapter. For one who is 'not delivered', the assertion 'I am *Brahma*' is the expression of an 'unreal' knowledge, that is to say, a knowledge that is purely speculative and theoretical, and not yet *realized* for him, even though what this 'unreal' knowledge expresses is always supremely real in itself. The consideration of this distinction between Reality (or Truth) in itself, on the one hand, and what we may call 'reality-for-me' on the other, must, in our opinion, permit an understanding of why unconsciousness, or, if preferred, ignorance (not speculative, but *real,* in the sense in which we have already used this word) of the Self cannot constitute a valid objection against the hypothesis here under examination.

Another difficulty, this time of the moral order, and, it would seem, more serious, is that if the hypostatic union is the truth of the

3. Luke 2:52.

human condition, then when man sins, God sins.[4] Now as sin consists essentially in an *aversio a Deo* [turning away from God], it is obviously impossible that God could sin, because, being perfectly One and very Unity, He cannot turn away from Himself. In this connection we may note that the Son, being pure relation to the Father—entirely *ad Patrem* in all that He is—is literally the *Anti-sin*, which fully justifies His title and mission of Redeemer. The title we have given this chapter thus requires completion, and we should specify that Jesus is like unto men in all *except sin*. But is this not to say in different terms that Jesus is not in all respects like men, all of whom in their real, concrete, and historical condition—excepting the Virgin Mary—are sinners? The absolute *impossibility* of sinning is clearly a direct, immediate, and necessary consequence of the hypostatic union, that is to say, it is personal. How then can the hypostatic union be the truth of man, of every man? It is clearly evident that in the matter of sin, personal responsibility on the part of God is to be rejected absolutely.

We are thus led to examine an analogous difficulty bearing on what classical theology calls the divine *concurrence*. We already alluded briefly to this in the first chapter, when we considered the concept of creation. There we wrote that of myself I have only the interior act by which I adhere and consent to moral evil recognized as such. God still does everything, because evil has no *being* as such, and 'everything that happens is worthy of adoration.' Certainly this does not absolve man of complete responsibility for his actions. To force the issue a little, we could even go so far as to say that in evil, man's responsibility is engaged more than in the good, since evil is what pertains specifically to him. This is expressly stated in the Benedictine Rule, which says, 'If one sees good in oneself, attribute it to God, not to oneself. As for evil, one knows that one is always the

---

4. Theologically, we cannot in fact conceive of a hypostatic union other than as effective from the first instant of conception, for otherwise, once it was realized, we would have not union, but a substitution of person. Cf. *Enchiridion Symbolorum*, Herder, 1967, Denziger no. 402: *non antea existente carne, et postea unita Verbo, sed in ipso Deo Verbo initium, ut esset, accipiente* (not the flesh first existing, and then the Word, but [the flesh] having its ontic origin in God the Word Himself).

author, and attributes it to oneself.'[5] In passing, let us observe in this connection how strange it is that the author of these lines is sometimes suspected of semi-Pelagianism. And here let us relate an interesting account from the teaching of Ramakrishna. Someone asked him, 'If God always inspires my actions, am I responsible for my sins?' The Sage responded, 'Duryodhana (a figure in Hindu Scripture, who is a kind of personification of evil) also said, "O Lord, Thou remainest in my heart and I do all that Thou makest me do!" But he who is persuaded that God alone acts and that he himself is only the instrument in His hand, cannot sin. A perfect dancer never makes a false step. As long as your heart is not purified, you cannot really believe in the existence of God.'[6] Two things seem particularly worthy of mention in this text. To believe truly in the existence of God is, for Ramakrishna, to believe in the divine action within us for the good. And the comparison with the dancer who makes a false step recalls St Thomas, for whom the sinner is like a man who walks (and this is entirely from God), *but with a limp.*[7]

Still, the difficulty remains real. When a criminal kills his victim, he sins, but whatever the act has of *being*, is from God, the universal first Cause, and without Him, the criminal could not act. Must we then hold God responsible for an act in which He 'concurs', and without whom it would not be? The question is far from pointless, and we know that the difficulty raised by the presence of evil, moral as well as physical (sometimes this latter seems more scandalous because it results from the nature of things), is often put forth by our contemporaries as an argument in favor of atheism. There is certainly no question of equating divine 'concurrence' with *personal* activity, but it is clear nonetheless that the two difficulties are not without a certain analogy. The responses, too, must also be analogous to a certain degree. For the moment we say only that in the non-dualist perspective, the man who sins, *sins against his own divine truth.*

---

5. *Rule of St Benedict*, chap. iv, 'What are the instruments for acting well?', Instruments nos. 42 and 43.

6. Ramakrishna, *L'Enseignement de Ramakrishna*, ed. Jean Herbert (Paris: Albin Michel, 1972), p436, n1339.

7. *Summa Theologica*, 1aP, Q49, a2 to 2m; cf. Q105, a5, *Utram Deus operetur in omni operante* (whether God works in every agent); cf. also IaIIae, Q6, a1 to 3m.

But let us return to the difficulty confronting us. If the hypostatic union is the truth of man, when man sins, God sins; or, more briefly still, the sinner is God! Can this be overcome? We can begin by returning to the logical distinction made earlier between a proposition understood in a composite sense and one understood in a divided sense. The assertion, 'The sinner is God', is monstrous if we attempt to understand it in the composite sense, but except for its particularly offensive ring, it becomes acceptable if we understand it in the divided sense. It is in fact a traditional assertion, that God became man in order that man the sinner might become God. Contrary to the way in which we applied it to the condition of contingent existence, here we find ourselves in the presence of a division resulting from a change effected in becoming, as in the classic example, 'the blind see', and with identical significance, since sin is naturally symbolized by corporeal blindness, particularly in the fourth Gospel. The sense of the proposition then becomes, '*The* (same man who was a) *sinner is* (become) *God*. This is an initial response, but it remains insufficient for two reasons. First, because the traditional assertion that God became man in order that man might become God, does not have the absolute sense wherein God is the *identity* of man. We should in fact note that the word 'God' is ambiguous, in that it can be understood either as a name of a person or a nature. Used as an attribute, it often has this latter meaning; used as a subject, it always has the first. This response is also insufficient for another reason, which is that to hypothesize a hypostatic union as the truth of man would mean that the man who sins is *already* God, independent of any subsequent becoming.

We said above that from the non-dualist perspective the man who sins does so against his own divine truth. This way of seeing the matter suggests another response. Rather than being considered the result of a becoming, the division between the subject (man as sinner) and predicate (God), will now be considered the result of ignorance: man is in truth God, but he does not know it, and this is why he sins. This new response is interesting, and appears more satisfying than the first; it reflects a view familiar to all the Orient, where the sequence 'Ignorance' (*avidyā*), 'Desire' (*kāma*), 'Action' (*karma*), is traditional in Hinduism as well as Buddhism. It is not yet fully sufficient, however, at least as long as the passage from Ignorance to Knowledge is considered a becoming. In fact, it seems to impute ignorance to God Himself, which is no more acceptable than to impute sin to Him.

It cannot be repeated often enough that in God there is no becoming. 'Every best gift, and every perfect gift, is from above, coming down from the Father of lights, with whom there is no change, nor shadow of alteration.'[8] Consequently, one does not *become* God. Non-dualist doctrine cannot be clearer on this point: once the Supreme Identity is attained, nothing is produced, nothing is changed. In this connection we can recount the testimony of Ramana Maharshi, a contemporary sage whom Hindus regard as a *jivan-mukta*, or one delivered in this life. When someone asked him, 'When were you delivered?' he answered, 'Nothing has happened to me; I am as I am.' His biographer, Dr Sarma Lakshman, maintained that in Ramana Maharshi's eyes, no one was in ignorance or servitude.[9] The 'passage'—or what appears as such—from ignorance (*avidyā*) to Knowledge (*vidyā*), *which is this very realization, is not a becoming*, and the same is true of the passage from non-existence to existence in creation. It goes without saying that the ignorance here in question is not simple theoretical ignorance of the rational order, but what might be called 'metaphysical ignorance', or again, 'real ignorance', in the sense in which we have just used this adjective. Like sin, this ignorance has no *being* and is without *origin*. In this sense, Hindu doctrine speaks of 'anterior non-existence' (*prāg-abhāva*).[10]

On the other hand, we must avoid imagining Deliverance as a kind of 'transubstantiation' of the human into the divine more or less along the lines of the change effected by the Eucharistic consecration. Nothing, in our opinion, could be further from the authentic Vedantic position. In the last chapter we already noted that, whereas the consecration effects a change, the Supreme Identity is

---

8. James 1:17.

9. Sarma Lakshman, *Étude*, in *Études sur Ramana Maharshi*, ed. Jean Herbert, Adyar (Paris: Dervy-Livres, 1949) [no page given].

10. *VCM*, vv. 198–199.

not the product of a non-preexisting result. The difference, seemingly of little importance at first glance, is in reality of considerable consequence. Indeed, from both Hindu and Christian points of view it is unthinkable that the supreme Principle could be conceived as a result or as the end of any change whatsoever, whether this change be human or cosmic. We mention this last point because some people, in their desire to escape the danger of anthropomorphism, fall into a no less fatal 'cosmomorphism'. Anthropomorphism and cosmomorphism are like the Scylla and Charybdis of the knowledge of God (it seems to us that Fr de Lubac said this somewhere). The declaration that God is the ultimate End, just as He is the first Principle, has a completely different meaning. It remains no less true that God is really the universal End (without end), and not the end of minds alone, for there is a necessary analogical correspondence between the End and the Beginning. 'I am Alpha and Omega, the beginning and the end, saith the Lord God, who is, and who was, and who is to come, the Almighty.'[11] However little we may reflect on this, does it not suggest that the ultimate End is not solely concerned with knowledge and love, at least not in the specific sense given these terms in Western philosophy and theology? This does not of course imply any adherence to the particular and somewhat hybrid 'views' of Fr Teilhard de Chardin.

> For the expectation of the creature waiteth for the revelation of the sons of God. For the creature was made subject to vanity, not willingly, but by reason of him that made it subject, in hope: because the creature also itself shall be delivered from the servitude of corruption, into the liberty of the glory of the children of God. For we know that every creature groaneth and travaileth in pain, even till now.[12]

We are insistent on this point, that it is at the level of the Infinite (insofar as it is permissible to speak of 'level' as regards the Infinite), and only at this level, that the following is realized, or rather, is found to be eternally realized, eternally real, without the subsistence

11. Rev. 1:8.
12. Romans 8:19–22.

of the least residue of dualism: *the total and perfect identity of Knowledge and Being.* TOTAL KNOWLEDGE IS TOTAL BEING; SUCH IS THE PERFECTION OF THE DIVINE ESSENCE. *Satyam Jñānam Ānantam Brahma*; the Supreme principle is Truth, Knowledge, Infinity. This is exactly what we wished to express when we said, 'God is Identity'. *Ex necessitate sequitur quod ipsum ejus (Dei) Intelligere sit ejus Essentia et ejus Esse* (It necessarily follows that His act of understanding must be His Essence and His Being).[13] From this perspective we say that in St John's Gospel, the Holy Spirit is called 'Spirit of Truth',[14] that is, He supereminently verifies in Himself the scholastic definition of truth as *adequatio rei et intellectus* (the adequation of the thing and the intellect), as He is Himself *adequatio Patris et Filii* (the adequation of the Father and the Son). It is in Him and by Him that the Son bears witness: 'I and the Father are One.'[15]

If Deliverance should not be represented as a kind of 'transubstantiation', how then should it be conceived? This question was already answered implicitly in the first chapter when we spoke of 'false imputation' or 'superimposition' (*adhyāsa*), which gives birth to the chain of existences (*samsāra*), of which the classic Indian example is the man who takes a rope for a serpent. It is this symbolism that we must now examine.

---

13. *Summa Theologica*, IaP, Q 14 a4.
14. John 14:17; 15:26; 16:13; cf. 1 John 5:6 AV, 'because the Spirit is Truth.'
15. John 10:30.

4

WITHOUT ME YOU
CAN DO NOTHING

SO A MAN ERRONEOUSLY takes a rope for a serpent. What happens? Nothing happens. The rope remains a rope and there is no serpent. If another man happens to pass by, he might say to the first man, 'Do not be afraid; the serpent you see *is* a rope.' And if the latter, no longer deluded, recognizes that it really is and always has been a rope that is in question, what happens? Again, nothing happens. *There will not be a serpent changed into a rope, for there never was a serpent.* Such, according to the Vedānta, is the identity of the world with all that it contains, and of *Brahma*, which—and let us not weary of returning to this point—is not the Creator or the 'Producer', *Brahmā*, distinct from his creation or his productions, *but the Infinite, that is to say, That outside of which there is nothing,* or rather which has neither outside nor inside. The world IS *Brahma* as the serpent IS a rope, just as the finite and the multiple IS, *in absolute Reality,* the Infinite without dualism. It is this concept which permits us to transpose the logical notion of 'divided sense' (*sensu diviso*) to make it express, beyond all becoming, the paradox of contingent existence (apparently) exterior to the Infinite. Indeed, just as the proposition 'the serpent is a rope' does not express an identity between a serpent and a rope because in reality there is no serpent, so likewise the assertion that 'the world *is Brahma*' does not express an identity between the manifested or apparent world and *Brahma*, because the apparent world, *apart from the Infinite,* is 'illusory', and this includes man-in-the-world with which I *fatally* (in both senses of the word) identify myself.[1] It is important to note that this is in no way a question of an *individual* illusion, a sort of hallucination, that is to say confusion between a reality of the psychic order and a reality of the sensory order. To understand the matter in this way would be to take literally the comparison of the man who mistakes a rope for a serpent and, as we have already had occasion to note in connection with the phenomenon of reflection, *to take the symbol for the thing symbolized. Māyā is a cosmic principle.* Here, again, as with the phenomenon of reflection, it is because they have suffered confusion of this kind that some people have assumed they could speak of the 'subjectivism' of the Vedānta. However, if no subjectivism whatsoever is involved, does this not lead back to simple monism? In no way, unless one wishes to characterize as monism the assertion that there is nothing outside the Infinite, which assertion cannot be contested.

In the first chapter we distinguished between substantiality and aseity. In Christian theology *Aseity* is that which corresponds least inadequately to the Vedantic notion of *Reality.* In fact, just as the 'visualized' serpent is not something that exists as such and independently, but all the reality imputed to it derives from the rope, so also the world is not something that exists as such and independently, and all the reality imputed to it, *that is to say the appearance of aseity in which, in our view, it is clad (and which is the basis for all atheism),* comes from the Divine Reality which lends it existence and which alone is *a Se.* Do we really grasp this intuition with its spiritual impact, in all its profundity? The comparison of the rope and the serpent indicates that the serpent is not pure imagination, without basis, for *if there were no rope, nothing would be seen.* It is the rope which one *mistakes for* the serpent because the rope lends the serpent all its apparent reality (the image of the dreamer, which we shall study below, proceeds from another point of view).

The doctrine of non-dualism does not annihilate the creature as such anymore than it deifies him. It simply asserts that the creature is entirely a *projection* or an 'expression' of the Divine Reality and that it is nothing *in and of itself.* 'The entire Universe is but the effect of *Brahma,* unique Reality. That is its veritable substance and the

---

1. In sum, the illusory nature of the world lies in this, that it presents itself to our awareness as an *absolute* reality.

world does not exist independently of That.'[2] It is this idea which authorizes us to draw a parallel between the ideas of creation *ex nihilo* and cosmic illusion, without being unfaithful to Shankara's thought. In fact, for Shankara, '*Māyā*, usually considered as cosmic illusion, *is also the very Power (Shakti) of the Lord.*'[3] We would say that this power by which He creates, that is to say, projects an exterior reality which manifests Him even in hiding Him, is so to speak the expansion of the *active Possibility* of all beings which we mentioned when we dealt with creation *ex nihilo*, possibility not really being distinguished from the divine Essence itself. One will grasp the importance of this verse for a correct understanding of Shankarian non-dualism. The 'illusory' character of the manifested world is expressly confirmed as having a 'non-human' origin and as the effect of the divine Power, *which means that only the divine Power can liberate from it.* This last remark will provide the occasion to answer a reproach currently voiced by some Christians against *Advaita Vedānta*.

We hear it said that this doctrine (and in a way the document of the Secretariat for Non-Christians is an echo of this) is fundamentally perverse and anti-Christian because it makes man a God and, in addition, implies a total confusion between the natural and supernatural orders. Conversely, one might think that if today so many Westerners are attracted to the East it is because they, too, attribute to the East this perversion and this confusion which in reality are nothing but the projection and reflection of their own uneasy tendencies and disordered aspirations. This is the sense in which we spoke of a 'luciferian vertigo' in the first chapter. A genuine discernment of spirits is thus necessary, and this is one of the reasons we were moved to write the present work. Indeed, we think that today it is of the greatest importance to make known what the doctrine of non-dualism really is, and thereby to cut short all false interpretations which derive either from insufficient or erroneous

---

2. *VCM*, v. 230. [The various English translations of the *Vivekacudamani* available to us follow slightly different numberings, some matching the numbering used here, some at variance with it. We note the verse as the author cites it. TRS].

3. *VCM*, v.108.

information or from passional blindness—or, to speak as did St Paul in circumstances not without analogy to our own, from a zeal 'not according to knowledge.'[4]

We can begin by recalling the document by the Secretariat for Non-Christians cited in the foreword. 'He (the Christian) will refrain, for example, from *a priori* rejecting as necessarily and totally monist and anti-Christian the ideal of identification with the Absolute which dominates Indian spirituality (*tat tvam asi*, thou art That, that is to say, the Absolute) and Islamic mysticism (*anā'l Haqq*, I am the Real, God—al-Hallaj).

The mention of al-Hallaj, tortured and put to death in Baghdad in 922 on the charge of having identified himself with God, is particularly interesting. We should not, of course, make the Secretariat document say more than it actually does, but it is nevertheless true that it constitutes an invitation for us not to hasten to condemn as anti-Christian a doctrine which, it must be acknowledged, was for a long time generally and uncontestedly considered in precisely this way.

If we may be permitted to express a criticism regarding the Secretariat document, we would say that Indian non-dualism, is rather a *doctrine of identity with the Absolute* than 'an ideal of identification with the Absolute' (the reader will already have noted this if he has followed us thus far). It is true that in principle the word 'identification' admits both meanings, *to recognize* and *to render* identical, but linked as it is here with 'ideal', it suggests the second. Now in this latter sense it is completely futile to wish 'to be identified with the Absolute,' which would not be the Absolute if we could become it. Vladimir Lossky was quite correct to write that 'one does not "find" God by 'seeking' Him from the starting point of a reality other than Himself.'[5]

For the non-dualist the Supreme Identity is not an 'ideal' towards which we might tend, and which we endeavor to attain. Even if not yet realized from a particular and quite relative (and fundamentally

4. Rom. 10:2.

5. Vladimir Lossky, *Théologie negative et connaissance de Dieu chez Maître Eckhart* (Paris: Vrin, 1973, 2nd ed.), p217.

'illusory') point of view, *it is the actual Truth of all existing things, and there is no other, for outside the Infinite there is nothing.* Once again, not identity *sensu composito*, in the composite sense, of the world and *Brahma* (of the serpent and the rope), but Identity which is not other than *Brahma* Itself, the Infinite without dualism, in Which in the final analysis every apparently extra-divine existence (*existens = extra stans*) is resolved (we do not say dissolved). It is not the identity of *two things*, but Identity transcending all dualism whatsoever, even including the dualism Creator-creature, both of these having been declared illusory as such *with regard to the Infinite.* To say the same thing in another way, *the Supreme Mystery infinitely transcends Its aspect as 'The Creator'.*

In the preceding, we have continually spoken of the Infinite, and indeed, this leads to a second criticism which we permit ourself concerning the document of the Secretariat for Non-Christians, that in speaking of the Absolute it was considered necessary to conform the document to general usage. We have already alluded to the serious drawbacks resulting from the use of the term 'Absolute' to render the word *Brahma*. Here we should explain this clearly. Briefly, 'Absolute' and 'relative' are two terms which *exclude one another.* The Vedantic doctrine of non-dualism as interpreted by Shankara, teaches that *Brahma* is the *unique* Reality; if this term is translated by 'the Absolute' we will inevitably be led to the conclusion that the relative, that is, the created world as a whole, is purely and simply non-existent. It will then be quite easy to reject a doctrine so manifestly irreconcilable with the Christian faith. In the first chapter we recalled that while creation is really distinct from the Creator, there is not more of *being* (singular), creation being included, than when it is excluded. The antinomy, which is completely eliminated by use of the word 'Absolute' as an equivalent to *Brahma*, is preserved if we speak of the Infinite instead of the Absolute. In fact, if there is obviously a *distinction* between the finite and the Infinite, this latter by definition (rather by 'infinition'), *comprehends everything* and leavings nothing outside Itself. However, we must avoid the too common error or misunderstanding of conceiving the Infinite as a totality formed by the addition of parts. The true Infinite is without parts (*akhanda*); otherwise stated, *the finite is not part of the Infinite.*

In order to demonstrate this more clearly we borrow here from the very simple reasoning of Bahya Ibn Pakuda.[6] Suppose that the Infinite is composed of parts, and we withdraw one of these parts. The remainder obviously will no longer be infinite. If we now add to this finite remainder the finite part we previously took from it, we see immediately that the total, the so-called infinite from which we started, is really not infinite but finite. We hope that our concern to specify as precisely as possible the exact meaning of the terms we employ, will not be taken as a pointless digression. In the course of our study, moreover, we will have further occasion to do this. Nicholas of Cusa wrote:

> Lord, my God, strength of the weak, I see that you are the infinite itself; therefore nothing is alien to you, nothing is different from you, nothing is opposed to you. The infinite is incompatible with otherness, for nothing can exist outside of it. . . . Thus the infinite is at once everything and nothing at all. No name is suitable for it, for every name can have a contrary, and nothing can be contrary to the unnameable infinite. It is not a whole opposed by parts, and it cannot be a part. . . .[7]

We have already said, and we say yet again, that *there is no true identity save in God, because God alone is Identity.* If we consider Christ Himself, his identity does not result from the union of the divine and human natures (in the way in which the identity of each human individual results from the union of soul and body), but *after, as well as before the incarnation*, this Identity is properly the eternal Word of the Father. *No one is perfectly identical to himself but God alone. He alone is He who is.*

We have said that the formula 'God is Identity' was inspired by our Christian faith. Indeed, we see indubitable affinities between the Hindu doctrine of *Identity* and the Christian Revelation of the *Trinity*, but this raises the question of the 'supernatural' character of the

---

6. Bahya Ibn Pakuda, *Les Devoirs du Cœur*, trans. André Chouraqui (Paris: Desclée De Brouwer), 1972.

7. Nicolas of Cusa, *Traité de la Vision de Dieu*, Louvain (Paris: Éditions du Museum Lessianum, 1925), pp 60–61.

Hindu doctrine. To begin with, let us immediately say *a priori* that we do not see any reason why we would be authorized to deny God the faculty of revealing Himself in one way or another outside the juridical frontiers of the institutional Church, as long as such a revelation did not contradict His total Revelation in Jesus Christ. It seems to us that such exclusivism would too closely recall the attitude of intransigent zealotry attributed to Joshua in the book of Numbers at the moment when a young boy ran in announcing to Moses that two men were prophesying in the camp. Joshua said, 'My lord Moses, forbid them! But he said: Why hast thou emulation for me? O that all the people might prophesy, and that the Lord would give them his Spirit.' [8]

So much for the question of *law*. As for the question of fact, we acknowledge that we have neither the means nor the authority which would permit us to resolve it. All that we wish to do here is to offer some reflections which, so we hope, may contribute however imperfectly and indirectly to laying the groundwork for a later examination of the problem. We will therefore leave to one side the question of whether or not the Vedantic doctrine of non-dualism may be regarded as 'revealed by God' in the specifically Christian sense of this expression, and limit ourself to showing that at least in a broad sense it does not lack the qualifications to be characterized as 'non-human'. We will speak to three of these qualifications: its metacosmic perspective, the 'faith' which it demands of its adherents, and the futility of all worldly means vis-à-vis the supreme Aim which it places before its followers. We could add that it presents itself as 'revealed' or, more precisely, as having been 'heard', if this would count for a non-Hindu, but if it does not, then it is at least a reason to question, and then to ascertain as far as possible, whether or not this contention is well founded—without, moreover, losing sight of the fact that there are revelations and revelations. And we can already add certain words of John Paul II, words which, before being inserted into an encyclical, cannot but have been carefully weighed:

8. Num. 11:27–29.

the strength of belief on the part of members of non-Christian religions—*this too, the effect of the Spirit of Truth operating beyond the visible frontiers of the visible Mystical Body*—should shame those Christians so often brought to doubt truths revealed by God and announced by the Church.[9]

The metacosmic, or if preferred, acosmic character of *Advaita Vedānta* is sufficiently evident from all that has been expounded up to this point. The following is a particularly clear statement by Shankara in this regard:

The steadfast conviction that *Brahma* is the only Reality and that the universe is illusory is what is called discrimination (*viveka*) between the Real and the unreal.[10]

Again, this sounds monist if we do not keep in mind that *Brahma* is the Infinite, so that the statement calls for the following paraphrase:

The steadfast conviction that the Infinite alone is *a Se* [from itself] (or, rather, since the Infinite cannot be positively characterized, *non ab alio* [not from another]) and that as such the finite, like the indefinite which is a only a development thereof, is illusory with regard to the Infinite, this is what is called discrimination between the real and the unreal.

We should add that formulas of this kind need to be balanced and clarified by others from the same author, which complete and in some measure correct them. At the beginning of this chapter we cited verse 230 where it is said that the entire universe is the effect of *Brahma*. The use of the word 'effect' clearly indicates that the universe is not regarded as a simple non-entity. If understood in this way, verse 138 can be cited in support of the same interpretation. 'He who is subject to ignorance mistakenly takes something for what it is not. Lacking discrimination, one sees a serpent in place of a rope. But serious dangers threaten the imprudent man who, misled by this erroneous notion, puts his hand on the serpent. Listen, my

---

9. *Redemptor hominis*, n.6, in *Documentation Catholique*, vol. 76 (1979), col. 304.
10. *VCM*, v. 20.

friend! It is man himself who puts himself in fetters because, in his ignorance, he views as real things which have only an ephemeral existence'. Two points in particular merit our consideration here. On the one hand, 'real' is not opposed to 'unreal' or to 'illusory', but to 'ephemeral; and on the other, to place one's hand on the (illusory) serpent entails serious (real) dangers. The substitution of 'ephemeral' for 'illusory' merits a pause of some length.

In order to link the following with our discussion above concerning the Infinite, let us observe at the outset that what is finite cannot exist of itself. Everything finite necessarily has an origin, whether this be a-temporal, as in the hypothesis of a creation *ab eterno*, or temporal, and is itself subject to the temporal condition. Only the Infinite has no principle and is eternal. But what is time? Let us attempt to answer this question, supposing it to be possible. We immediately note that we do not consider time as 'measure of movement', according to the classical and somewhat exterior and 'mechanical' definition, but rather in its fundamental phenomenon, the incessant succession of 'nows' that cannot be added (they are fused only in our psyche), that are not compossible, excluding one another so that one alone *is* in each of the moments of my life, narrowly enclosing this life in a kind of tight and moving prison. Here let us quote St Augustine:

> We say 'this year', but what do we have of this year outside the present day? For of this year, the days gone by are already past and the days to come are not yet here. We are in a given day and we say 'this year'. Say rather 'today' if you would speak of something present. ... But if you say 'today', I would say: Once again observe that the first hours of this day are past and the hours to come not yet here. Correct that also, and say 'at this very hour'. But of this hour, what do you have? Certain of its moments are already past, and the moments to come are not yet here. 'In this very moment', do you say? But what moment? While you express

these syllables, if you enunciate two, the second does not sound until the first is already past. This very syllable, finally, if it has two letters, the one does not sound until the other has gone. What do you have, therefore, of these years...? [11]

If we do not want our analysis of temporal succession to risk seeming unintelligible, we must warn the reader against a natural inclination of the Western mind to imagine that the differentiation of its concepts corresponds to a real separation in things. If we are considering time, for example, we spontaneously tend to picture it to ourselves as a sort of reality in itself, separable from its flowing content (which includes ourselves). It is thus almost inevitable that many things remain so closed to us that we cannot even see them. Certainly it is legitimate and even necessary to analyze, to take apart and distinguish, but on condition of not being duped, and of always ensuring that the *intelligence*, the faculty of *being*, and not reason alone (which knows only relationships), does not lose contact with the *unity* of the real.

It will not be inappropriate at this point to say a few words about the famous argument of Zeno of Elea concerning Achilles and the turtle, and although it may seem to be a digression, our sole aim is to illustrate the above reflections. The sophism is well known. As handed down to us, Achilles, having set out to catch a turtle, could never reach it. This is a typically Greek kind of problem—or rather pseudo-problem—which, in our view, would never occur to a Semite, in particular. To show its fallacious character, let it suffice to schematize the data. At the speed of 2 meters per second, runner A pursues another, B, who in the same time runs only a meter. The distance which separates them is 2 meters. Allegedly it is demonstrated that runner A will never overtake runner B. The argument goes that when A will have covered the 2 meters and reached B's original point, B will have moved away from it by 1 meter. Then, when A will have covered this meter, B will have moved ahead 50

---

11. Augustine, *In Psalmorum*, 76.8 [Cited in A.K. Coomaraswamy, *Temps et Éternité* (Paris: Dérvy-Livres, 1976), p97; English original, *Time and Eternity* (Ascona, Switzerland: Artibus Asiae Publishers, 1947), p113. TRS].

centimeters. These 50 centimeters being covered, B will be found 25 centimeters ahead, and so forth, so that the distance separating the two runners, always diminishing by half, will never be reduced to nothing. A will never overtake B.

How is it not seen that all the apparent strength of this sophism comes from the failure to consider the time factor?

We should thus alter our statement, introducing the factor of time. It goes without saying that the problem as posed presumes that the speed of A and that of B remain constant, that is to say, that in the span of one second the distance run by A will be always 2 meters and the distance run by B will always be 1 meter. Our statement is completed as follows: when, *in 1 second,* A will have covered the 2 meters separating him from B, B will have advanced 1 meter. When A will have covered this meter, *in half a second,* B again will have covered 50 centimeters. When A will have covered 50 centimeters, *in a quarter second,* B will have moved away 25 centimeters, and so forth. *What leaps to our attention is that there are indefinitely diminishing times corresponding to the indefinitely diminishing distances:* 1 second + a half second + a quarter second, and so on, so that what the reasoning really proves is that A will never reach B... *until two seconds have elapsed.* It is hard to believe that this could have gone unnoticed.[12]

Let us now resume our consideration of succession. In each successive moment of time, *now,* there is the world, and simultaneously, in an eternity without succession which is not other than Himself, God. World and time are not separate realities. The world is not on one side, and the present moment, apart from the world, on the other. There is a unique existent which we may call 'the world-now'. In each of the minutes of my life, in this instant in which I write these lines (and this instant in which I am read), *nothing else has existence.* The 'world-of-the-preceding-now' has passed, disappeared, vanished in the 'world-of-the-present-now' which has just succeeded it. I can go in search of it, go anywhere I wish, but I can be sure that I will not find it anywhere. *It does not*

---

12. Of course what we say here is valid only for this form of the sophism, and not for those in which time is not a consideration.

exist. Its very recollection, which is the trace of it in my memory, is a *present* recollection, a part of the 'world-now' from which I am absolutely forbidden to escape (*except perpendicularly in relation to time, by the narrow gate of the instant present which opens directly on eternity*), and which, in its turn will totally pass away—which is even now passing away, because *to be passing* is its very essence— to be replaced by a new 'world-now' which succeeds it without the least break in continuity, and so on indefinitely. What we say here of the world in general also applies to 'man-in-the-world', whom we may call by the name given him by Jesus in the nocturnal conversation with Nicodemus, 'that which is born of the flesh.' We also cite Plutarch, 'Dead is the man of yesterday, for he had died into the man of today; and the man of today is dying in the man of tomorrow.'[13]

It is clear that this is not a matter of reflections on the 'brevity of life'. *Life is neither long nor brief. I taste only one moment at a time. My life is this present moment.* From this arises the sentiment we sometimes experience, however little we pause to observe ourselves and our ambience, of *beginning to exist now*, of *being* for the first time, and at the same time—strangely—of *never having been born*. We will see the exact significance of this 'impression' further on, when we speak of 'pseudo-aseity', but for the moment we can say that this in no way suppresses continuity in our life, but that as a Buddhist might say, it is a 'continuity without identity'. *Identity is not situated at the level of temporal existence.*

We can recall in this connection the Sufi doctrine of the 'renewal' of creation at each (divine) breath which, despite the great differ- ence of form, is in fundamental agreement with Hindu teaching on the true Self. Muhyi-d-Din ibn al-'Arabi, whom the Sufis consider as the greatest of spiritual masters, expounds this doctrine as fol- lows, 'Man does not realize that he is not and that he is anew with each 'breath' (it is a question of the divine exhalation which 'dilates' the worlds from their state of non-manifestation). And if I say 'anew', I do not suppose any temporal interval but a purely logical succession. In the 'renewal of creation at each breath', the instant of

---

13. Plutarch, *Moralia* 392D, cited in Coomaraswamy, op. cit., p74.

annihilation coincides with the instant of manifestation of a like [creation]'.[14] Al-Qashabi comments thus on this passage:

> There is no temporal interval between annihilation and remani-festation, so that one does not perceive any interruption between the two analogous and successive creations, and their existence seems homogenous.... Insofar as man is a possibility of mani-festation but does not see what manifests him, he is pure absence ['*udum*, 'absence', 'non-existence']; on the other hand, insofar as he receives his being from the perpetual irradiation [*tajalli*] of the Essence, he *is*.[15]

It is easy to see that the irradiation in question is the same thing as the 'solar light' of Hindu symbolism mentioned in the first chapter.

We observed above that the 'world-of-the-preceding-moment' does not exist in the 'world-now'. We can now add that the 'world-now' itself, which is even now passing away, has no greater exist-ence. It is in effect a *past* that is to come, if such an expression is per-missible, a future *past*. Now, as Gaudapādacharya wrote, 'That which exists neither before nor after likewise does not exist now.' We thereby grasp how, in the Vedantic perspective, 'unreal' or 'non-exis-tent' and 'ephemeral' can in fact be identical. *It is important, never-theless, not to confuse the 'passing' and the 'present'*, as if in reality nothing could exist. Time, connoting unreality, is only the condi-tion of what *passes*. This is why the verb 'to pass' seems to us the most capable of designating each of these three 'parts' of time called past, present, and future in everyday language. Thus, for our part, we would say of the world understood as the ensemble of *passing things*, that it is first 'to pass' (it is the 'to-come'),[16] that it is then 'passing' *and not present*, and that finally it is 'past'. *The present is therefore not part of time.* [17] It is not 'of this world'. This is why at the

---

14. Muhyi-d-dīn Ibn 'Arabi, *La Sagesse des Prophètes*, translation and notes by Titus Burckhardt (Paris: Albin Michel, 1974), pp152–153.

15. Ibid., p153, n1.

16. The French is 'à-venir', whence 'avenir', which is the French for 'future'. TRS

17. Cf. Boethius, *De Trinitate*, IV: *Nunc fluens facit tempus, nunc stans facit aeter-nitatum* (The now that flows makes time, the now that stands makes eternity), cited by St Thomas, *Summa Theologica* 1aP, Q10, A2.

start of these reflections we took care to specify that at each moment of time, there is the world and, simultaneously, an eternity without succession which is not other than Himself, God. The true present is in fact that of eternity. *It does not pass.* It is only with regard to what passes that we can speak of succession, and therefore of time.

Praeterit enim figura hujus mundi, says the Apostle in the Latin Vulgate,[18] 'for the fashion of this world passeth away,' but it seems to us that what the Apostle is saying is much more profound and goes much further. We do not find it too far removed from an admission of a veritable equivalence between 'unreal' and 'ephemeral' as found in Shankara. In fact the term rendered in the *Vulgate* by *praeterit* is παραγει, and it is to be noted that the verb παραγω, used transitively, has equally the sense of 'seduce', 'deceive', or 'dupe'. Moreover, the word σχημα, rendered by *figura*, also has the sense of 'exterior', of 'appearance', and even of 'pretence'. The comparison of these two terms invites us, without forcing the text, to the translation, 'The appearance of this world is deceitful', which seems more in line with what preceded it, where St Paul exhorts the disciples of Jesus Christ not to let themselves be taken in by appearances and to 'use the world as not using it'. We can say likewise that the passage is in keeping with what he says elsewhere[19] of our world subject to 'vanity' (ματαιοτητι), especially if we follow certain linguists for whom the Greek ματη, 'something vain', is linked to the Latin *mentiri*.

We have said that we must take care not to confuse present and *passing*, and it is against precisely this illusion that the Apostle warns his readers. We have also compared the present moment to a narrow prison; we now say more explicitly—having already alluded to it briefly—that the present is also the 'place', and the only possible one, of our Deliverance, it being the very place of the eternal, which alone is truly 'instantaneous' (*instans*) and which involves no succession and therefore no annihilation. '*Now* is the acceptable time,' says St Paul.[20] It is to be noted that the Apostle uses the same word χαιροσ which he used at the beginning of his exhortation to 'use the

18. I Cor. 7:31.
19. Rom. 8:20.
20. II Cor., 6:2.

world as if not using it': 'Tempus (ὁ χαιροσ) *breve est*.[21] In fact, καιροσ does not designate time in general, but the moment, and especially the favorable moment, the occasion. The 'occasion' of salvation is restricted (συνεσταλμενος), just as the *passing* is confined between the future and the past. It must be seized at the moment of passage, and we could say very precisely that *the present moment is 'the Pascha of the Lord.'*[22] Here we have the foundations of a whole 'spirituality of the present moment', the profundity of which is seldom even suspected. 'Be aware that the place of Time is Eternity, that is to say, the Instant or the Present,' wrote Nicholas of Cusa.[23] And here we can recall the myth of the Symplegades (from the Greek συμπληγας, 'which crashes together'), the two rocks situated at the entrance to the Bosphorus in the Black Sea, which were said to strike together, crushing the ships which ventured between them.[24] The Symplegades represent the future and the past, between which must pass anyone hastening towards the present of eternity. The *passage* from the 'flesh' to the 'spirit' is truly instantaneous, as St Thomas expressly notes.[25] And here we will end these considerations called forth by the equivalence of the 'ephemeral' and the 'unreal', and continue our account.

Although from the point of view of the Infinite (if this expression has any meaning), the 'illusioned' is himself the 'illusion', it is no less true that from the point of view of creatures such as ourselves in our present state of manifestation, it is impossible without further ado to regard as 'unreal' the world that surrounds us, any more than we can so regard ourselves. Otherwise there would be nothing from which we ought to liberate ourselves, or even *any person to be*

21. I Cor., 7:29.
22. Cf. Exod. 12:11.
23. Nicolas of Cusa, *Où est le nouveau-né?*, *Œuvres choisies*, p467.
24. Coomaraswamy, op. cit., p44, n24.
25. *Summa Theologica*, IaIIae, Q113, a7: *utrum justificatio impii in instanti vel successive* (whether the justification of the impious is effected instantly or successively) [cited in Coomaraswamy, op. cit., p107. TRS].

liberated. Now, on the contrary, it is a fact that the capital virtue required of the aspirant to Liberation is the ardent desire to be liberated (*mumukshutva*)[26]. We would thus be strangely mistaken to conceive of non-dualism as a kind of Oriental quietism. It forcefully underlines the impossibility of 'realizing' the Supreme Identity without spiritual energy, determination, and moral courage (*titikshā*),[27] of which undoubtedly only very few are capable; and far from giving the impression that the Supreme Goal can be attained cheaply (even though it is quite near), it ceaselessly exposes the innumerable difficulties which accumulate before the aspirant, or rather *in him.* He is—we have already cited this traditional expression—'on the razor's edge', and the ardor with which he must aim towards Deliverance is compared to the impetuosity of the man who, his hair aflame, flings himself into a pond. Another no less striking image compares the patience required of a bird which might try to empty the ocean by soaking the tips of its wings, then going to the shore to shake them dry. All this shows that if from the point of view of Infinite Reality there can be neither slave nor servitude, from our present point of view it would be foolish to regard as 'illusory' efforts that can be undertaken to attain the Goal. However, once the Goal is attained, it will be apparent that the 'creature', recognized as illusory, will have played no role, *for Realization is not a possibility of the creature.*

All these apparent inconsistencies arise because, while things remain what they are in themselves, they are subject to consideration from different points of view, and of course the passage from one point of view to another distorts perspectives and displaces planes. There is something very important in this reflection and we must pause to consider it.

Whether it be of the East or West, a text expressing a judgment on the degree of 'reality' of the created order cannot possibly be interpreted correctly if the general point of view from which it arises has not been previously and precisely determined. We should consider this observation of capital importance, for failure to take it

26. *VCM*, v. 27.
27. *VCM*, v. 24.

into account can leave both proponents and adversaries of the doctrine of non-dualism open to unfortunate misunderstandings. We will distinguish three principal points of view.

First is the creature's point of view, which can be characterized as 'natural' in every sense of this word. It envisages all of creation according to its own composition and its concrete existence. Creation appears as in some way occupying an intermediary degree between the Creator, from Whom it receives its *being*, and the nothingness from which it seems to have come forth. Envisaged in this way, it is presented as an (impossible) mixture of being and non-being (in the privative sense). It is the reflection which, though participating to some degree in the reality of the object which it 'represents', nevertheless has only the empty appearance of this reality. Its 'reality' is essentially ambiguous. It is neither from itself nor permanent, all its reality being outside itself. Two verses of the *Vivekacudamani* already cited translate this manner of seeing: verse 230, 'The entire universe is only the *effect* of *Brahma*, the unique Reality . . . the world does not exist independently of That'; and verse 138, 'Man places himself in fetters because in his ignorance he regards as real things which have only an *ephemeral existence*.'

The second and third points of view are opposed to one another and are situated so to speak symmetrically on either side of the first. One viewpoint sees things from the perspective of God, the other from the perspective of 'nothingness'. 'God's point of view' is in turn divided into two according to whether creatures are seen either outside Him as 'projections' or 'expressions' of Himself (which is already a 'dualist' view of reality), or, more profoundly, according to whether God views them in the unity and simplicity of His Essence. We say that this point of view (insofar as it is permissible to speak of a point of view in this last case) is more profound because it expresses ultimate Reality less inadequately. God does not know beings 'from the outside' (which really makes no sense for God), in their apparently extra-divine existence, but in their Principle and Truth, which He Himself is. This last point of view (the 'second point of view of God') can be related to verse 226 of the *Vivekacudamani*:

Brahma is the Supreme Unity, the Unique Reality, because nothing other than the Self exists. For the one who has realized the Truth of truths, where would there be an entity other than *Brahma*, an entity independent of *Brahma*?

Concerning this point of view, we would like to make a remark which seems important to us. If, as St Thomas teaches, it is true—and it is necessary that it should be so—that God sees things not in themselves, in their exterior *being* as creatures, but in Himself, in His Essence, *non in ipsis, sed in seipso; inquantum essentia sua continet similitudinem aliorum ab ipso*[28] (not in themselves, but in Himself, in so far as His Essence contains the likeness of all that is other than Himself), then how can some declare that things are more truly themselves in their created *esse* than in the divine mind—stated otherwise, in their uncreated *esse*, since *creatura in Deo est ipsa essentia divina* (the creature in God is not other than the Divine Essence Itself)?[29] Does this not amount to attributing a certain imperfection or inadequation to the knowledge *per similitudinem* that God has of them, compared to the down to earth and 'such as they are' knowledge which other creatures have of them? Situating ourselves at the purely metaphysical point of view, this is why we say that the *truth* of creatures is in God, which was also the way Meister Eckhart saw the matter, namely, that *God is Truth*.

Finally, a third point of view considers creatures not 'in themselves', as did the first, nor in God, as did the second, but in what they would be if reduced to themselves (if, in these conditions, we can speak in this way), *God excluded*—in short, what subsists of the reflection when the [reflected] object is removed, that is to say, nothing at all. It is in this sense that we should understand the *purum nihil* of Meister Eckhart, condemned because of its ambiguity but shown to be perfectly orthodox when returned to its context. Meister Eckhart's only fault (admitting that it was one), was to want to strike his listeners forcefully and shake them up for the sake of an interiorized *metanoia*, to use abrupt and hard-hitting formulas,

---

28. *Summa Theologica*, IaP, Q14, A5.
29. Thomas Aquinas, *Quaestiones Disputatae de Potentia Dei*, 3, 16.

which he did in the following instance. *Omnes creaturae sunt unum purum nihil: non dico quod sint quid modicum vel aliquid, sed quod sint unum purum nihil* (All creatures are pure nothingness; I do not say that they are a little thing, but that they are pure nothingness).[30] In the first chapter we said that evil has no being. We can now say that sin consists precisely in attaching oneself (or in wanting to attach oneself) to one's 'own being' as creature, *God excluded*, that is to say—insofar as this might be possible—to that *purum nihil* of which Eckhart spoke with the greatest clarity:

> That which has no being is nothingness. All creatures lack being, *for their being depends upon the presence of God*.[31] If God should turn away from all creatures for an instant, they would vanish into nothingness. I have sometimes said, and it is quite true: he who would add the entire world to God would have nothing more than if he had God alone. Without God all creatures have no more being than a midge; without God, exactly as much, neither more nor less.[32]

This latter is Shankara's most usual perspective, conveyed thus by the already cited verse 20 of the *Vivekacudamani*: 'The steadfast conviction that *Brahma* is the only Reality and that the universe is illusory, this is what is called discrimination between the Real and the unreal.' We have said that this point of view is symmetrical with

30. Meister Eckhart, *Omne datum optimum*, in *Sermons*, trans. Jeanne Ancelet-Hustache (Paris: Editions du Seuil, 1974–78), vol. I, p 65.

31. St Thomas is of the same view, and, quite remarkably, in order to make his meaning clear, uses the image of the solar ray: *Hunc autem affectum* [i.e., *esse*] *causat Deus in rebus, non solum quando primo esse incipiunt sed quamdiu in esse consevantur: sicut lumen causatur in aere a sole, quamdiu aer illuminatus manet. Quamdiu igitur res habet essetamdiu oportet quod adsit ei* (God causes this effect in things, not only when they begin to be, but also as long as they are kept in being, as the sun causes the light in the air as long as the air remains illumined). 'As long as a thing has being, it is therefore necessary that God be present to it,' Summa Theologica 1aP, Q 8. In our own day, too, Vatican II: 'The creature without the Creator evaporates' (*Gaudium et Spes*, 36, 3). Is it not remarkable that this assertion is encountered in a document which is generally viewed as a kind of charter for an 'opening to the world'?

32. Meister Eckhart, op. cit.

what we have called the first of 'God's points of view'. This symmetry can be expressed as follows: just as, from God's perspective, there is no more *being,* creation included than excluded, so from the perspective of 'nothingness', there is no less *nothingness,* creation included (*God excepted*) than excluded. It is hardly necessary to add that in reality this last 'point of view' does not correspond to anything whatsoever.

This being the case, and following the point of view adopted, creation can always be envisioned either as 'exterior' to the Creator, or as eternally contained in Him who is its Principle and its End as also its actual and eternal Truth. If the first point of view is adopted, we must be careful not to let ourselves be deceived by the metaphorical character of the notions 'exterior' and 'interior' when these are applied to God or to the relation of creatures to God. Understood literally, they in fact designate spatial and *therefore created* qualifications, of which only the possibilities are in God (and are God) beyond any humanly conceivable mode *and without contrariety.* This is why in the second of these two points of view, that from which creatures are seen in God, we must take care to transpose beings 'outside' the conditions of existence which pertain to them as creatures, and to consider them in God 'in the condition of God'. There, in their permanent Truth and transcendent Identity, they are not really distinct one from another, nor really different, nor really multiple, but are perfectly simple and immutable Reality, uncreated and eternal, necessary and Divine, without the least real loss (except the apparent loss of their finitude), but [are] rather in the plenitude of their Being, unaffected by the apparently extra-divine character of their created *esse,* as the sun is not affected by its reflection, or the rope by the form of the serpent which is added to it. Here again we can quote Nicholas of Cusa:

Whoever would understand this simplicity of the infinite Unity, infinitely anterior to all opposition, where everything is enveloped independent of all composition, where neither alterity nor diversity enters, where man does not differ from the lion, nor heaven from earth, where nevertheless all things are present in the truest manner, not in their finitude, certainly, but constituting this very Unity that envelopes them.[33]

After this digression on the various points of view from which the real can be envisaged and to which we have been brought by Shankara's 'acosmism', we return to an examination of the Vedānta's claims to be 'non-human'. Our discussion of the last two claims will be much briefer, and we can begin immediately by noting that the three claims enumerated correspond respectively to the orders of being, truth, and goodness.

The second is the intellectual claim, and is merely the simple consequence of the first. Since Truth is transcendent, and things considered 'in themselves' are not truly real because all their reality is in God, all knowledge that we can have of these things will never be anything but the knowledge of an illusion. It is therefore radically incapable of making us know the real Truth. All human knowledge, whether scientific or philosophical, is rooted in sensible or psychic experience, and in using and manipulating these data, philosophical logic obviously lacks any common measure with transcendent Truth and can only efface itself before a truly adequate means, namely 'faith' (*shraddhā*), which alone permits apprehension of the Real. Shankara declares this expressly:

> By a deliberate act of understanding to adhere to Truth as expounded in the Scriptures and in the teaching of the spiritual Master—this is what the Sages designate by the term faith, *and by faith one understands the Real.*[34]

Given all that we have said, it hardly seems necessary to specify that in this context it would be wrong to speak of 'fideism'.

Finally, the third claim. Because only the Infinite is absolutely real, and because there is nothing outside the Infinite, or rather, as we have already emphasized, there is neither without nor within, since the Infinite is without either exterior or interior, no approach,

---

33. Nicolas of Cusa, *Du Nom divin et de la Théologie affirmative*, in *La Docte Ignorance*, trans. Louis Moulinier (Paris: Guy Trédaniel, Éditions de la Maisnie, 1979), c1930.

34. *VCM*, v 25.

no knowledge, no comparison, is possible *from without*. The same 'supra-naturalism' noted at the level of being, then at the level of knowledge, is inevitably found again at the level of effective 'realization"; 'grace' (*kripā*) necessarily responds to faith (*shraddhā*). 'Nothing,' Shankara asserts, 'can cut these bonds [of ignorance] but the marvelous sword of Knowledge forged by discrimination, when the edge has been whetted by divine Grace.' [35]

We have mentioned 'supra-naturalism', and should explain the term briefly. We think that the term 'supernatural' is too much identified with Christian theology, where it has a too precise and as it were technical sense to permit it to be applied to ways of envisaging things that are entirely foreign to this theology, even after many cautionary warnings and explanations. Let us recall briefly the historical origin of this idea which appears correlatively with and is defined in relation to that of 'nature' such as this was elaborated in classical Greek philosophy. Now it is quite well known, though all the consequences are seldom drawn, that the viewpoint of philosophy (restricting the term to its proper and precise sense) is an essentially 'profane' point of view, exclusive to a late period of the Hellenic world, and that it does not have its exact equivalent in other civilizations where the very idea that there could be an independent knowledge and reality can only be deemed a proof of pure ignorance and incomprehension.

Reserving therefore the use of the word 'supernatural' for what relates exclusively to the perspective of Christian theology, we will in preference speak of the 'supra-natural', and say that from the perspective of *Advaita Vedānta, the supra-natural order is closely identified with the Real*, while what we can call the 'natural' order is that of the 'illusory' and the 'profane'—in a word, of 'ignorance'. No doubt there is reason to include in the supra-natural order, and as an extension thereof, everything in the 'world of man' which presents itself as a direct manifestation of the pure supra-natural and as a movement towards it—in short, everything expressed by the word 'tradition' understood in the sense indicated, including its 'non-human' (*apaurusheya*) origin, the gage of its efficacy. We say then

35. Ibid., v147.

that the elements of tradition thus understood are, on the one hand, the 'revealed' (or more precisely, heard) scripture (*shruti*), that is to say, proceeding from an inspiration or from a direct intuition that is likened to an audition; and, on the other, the guru and the mantra, inseparable, as the one entails the other. And we will add that this pairing, while having its own character and originality, here plays a role analogous to that of the sacraments in Christian life, *mutatis mutandis*. It must be said, moreover, that this order of consideration too often escapes the individualism and practical 'naturalism' of the great majority of our contemporaries.

It is difficult to overestimate the importance of the rôle of the guru in Indian spirituality. Certainly, whether he is *jñānin* or *bhakta*, Shaivite or Vishnuite, there is no Hindu who does not know that the true guru (*sad-guru*) is the interior guru, that is to say the true Self (*Ātmā*) or such and such a particularized aspect of the Divinity (*ishta*), according to the perspective proper to each. But generally all admit, if not the necessity, at least the very great utility and convenience, of the exterior guru. They seek him ardently and perseveringly until, believing they have found the one divinely destined for them, they attach themselves to him and consecrate themselves more or less completely to his service. The human and exterior guru has no other *raison d'être* than to lead to the divine and interior Guru, with whom the human guru is identified. Shankara's *Vivekacudamani* opens with an invocation to *Govinda* addressed inseparably to his own guru, Govindapada, and to the divine *Govinda* himself, that is to say to *Krishna, avatara* of *Vishnu* and the Guru of gurus. We note in passing that something analogous is found in Christianity notably where the Rule of St Benedict opens similarly with an exhortation to a 'Father' who is doubtless both the Patriarch of monks and the Father in Heaven. The same treatise of Shankara ends with a song to the guru (*guru-gīta*) expressly asserting that

the guru is *Brahmā*, the guru is *Vishnu*, the guru is *Shiva* himself. In truth, the guru is the supreme *Brahma*. . . . It is by his grace (*kripā*) that the aspirant may realize the One who penetrates everything mobile or immobile in the universe. . . . It is He, the supreme *Ātman*. . . . It is within the guru that the universe has its beginning, but He is without beginning. The guru is the highest Divinity. None is superior to the guru. . . . It is He who gives the Vedic mantras such as: Thou art That.[36]

Although it is most often restricted to the Divine or human Master, sometimes the word guru extends to the designation of anything which in one degree or another vehicles a spiritual teaching and a corresponding grace, as witness for example verse 76 [of the *Viveka-cudamani*] enumerating as 'instructors' the deer, the elephant, the moth, the fish, the bee. Similarly, the *Uddhava-Gītā*:

> I have numerous instructors, O King, and, using my intelligence, I turned to all of them. I acquired this wisdom during my passage through the world, for I listened to all the messages conveyed to me by my instructors.[37]

The same idea is found in Tibet where Milarepa declared:

> By breaking, the earthenware vase which was my sole wealth has now become a guru, because it has provided an admirable discourse on impermanence.[38]

By our extensive inquiry into matters relating to basic traditional elements we have aimed to draw attention to a too much neglected aspect of Hinduism. In the West it is often claimed that the East has no interest in anything that is not pure 'spirituality', that its doctrine is, as is often said, 'disincarnate'. Now while this may have an indubitably acceptable sense, the way in which it is commonly understood does not always correspond with reality. Even in the most radical non-dualism there is room for what may be called in a purely indicative and analogical sense a 'sacramental order', that is to say, an ensemble of *signs* and *means* which are considered efficacious and

---

36. We have been unable to locate this song to the guru in the various editions of the *Vivekacudamani* we have consulted. TRS

37. *Uddhava-gita*, II, 32, cited in *VCM*, p21. [The English translations we have consulted render the second sentence differently. See, e.g., Swami Ambikananda Saraswati, *The Uddhava-gita* (Berkeley, CA: Seastone, 2002), p33. TRS]

38. *Vie de Milarepa* (Paris: Adrien Maisonneuve, 1955), p260.

which, though pertaining to daily existence and finding their support therein, are regarded as the *expression* and the *vehicle* of a Transcendence.

Let us close these reflections by saying again that it is often those who reproach the East for the so-called 'disincarnate' character of its spirituality who, seemingly without being aware of the illogicality of their position, criticize the excessive importance which they think it grants to psychosomatic techniques such as those of *yoga* —of which they misunderstand the aim. Criticizing also its 'idolatry', they are incapable of grasping its 'methodical' and 'provisional' character which is nevertheless attested to by traditional texts such as:

> It is in order to aid the contemplative prayer of worshippers that a form has been given to this *Brahman* which is pure Spirit, transcendent, and immaterial.[39]

In this connection and without risking scandal to Christians, may we be permitted to suggest that 'idolatry' (and we understand thereby the multiplication of 'gods' and their material or mental representations)[40] might play a rôle in Hinduism, taking account of profound differences in mentalities, analogous to a certain will to 'incarnation', understood in a broad sense, as a divine 'condescension' (we do not say indulgence) in regard to the multiple weaknesses inherent in the human condition—in brief a 'propaedeutic' and quasi pastoral rôle? And we will add that quite possibly this rôle was recognized and assumed in India in a much more conscious and deliberate manner than we would be inclined to permit in the Christian West. Whatever one's views on this matter we believe that in any case it would simply be wrong to compare Hindu 'idolatry' to the idolatry with which first the Jews then Christians may have been familiar in Palestine and in the Roman Empire. In this connection we will again cite another traditional Hindu text which will also serve as commentary:

---

39. Raghunananda, *Traité sur la consécration des statues*, cited by Fr Fallon in *La Priere*, [no page given].

40. These remarks could perfectly well be applied within Christianity itself to the Orthodox as regards their iconography. TRS

O Master of the universe, pardon the triple fault that my impotence has led me to commit: to Thee, who art beyond all form, my contemplation has given a form; my praises have made me forget Thine ineffable character; my pilgrimages to sacred places and temples have destroyed Thine omnipresence.[41]

Christians would not be ill advised to let such texts serve as inspiration and, at times, to make them an object of their meditation.

To close this chapter consecrated to the supra-natural character of Vedantic doctrine, and, at the same time, to link it to the following chapter, let us return a moment to the subject of the guru. We recalled that the unique *raison d'être* of the human and exterior guru is to lead to the divine and interior Guru, who is the true spiritual Master, and with which the former is identified. *In fact there is no other guru than the divine Word himself.* 'Neither be ye called masters; for one is your master, Christ.'[42] This why Shankara declared that 'it is in the guru that the universe had its beginning, but He is without beginning', which provides the occasion to pose once again the question asked at the end of the first chapter. May faith in a guru, identified with the divine Word and venerated as His human aspect, be accounted as an implicit faith in the Word made Man?

The divine word (*shabda-brahma*) is the primordial Sound (*pranava*), the sacred Syllable Om (*Om-kara*), Place and Principle of all manifestation (or creation) as of all Revelation (or audition). In the last resort there is no truly 'magisterial' function which is not in reality an effusion of and a participation in His divine authority:

The sovereign splendor conferred by the illumination of the Self, this have I received from the supreme majesty of Your grace. Salutations to You, O glorious Instructor! Noble-hearted being, salutation, and salutation without end! O my Guru, in a rush of compassion You awakened me from lethargy, and so doing have permanently assured my salvation! In an unending dream, I

41. Cited by Fr Fallon in *La Prière*, [no page given].
42. Matt. 23:10. [In the French original, the author quotes the verse only in part, as, 'You have but one Master, the Christ.' TRS]

wandered aimlessly, lost in this forest of birth, decay, and death created by illusion. I was long tormented by endlessly recurring afflictions, and was pursued without pity by a tiger, the sense of the *ego*. Salutation to You, O Prince of gurus! You whose greatness is inexpressible. *You are eternally identical to Yourself, and You manifest Yourself as the universe!* I prostrate myself at Your feet![43]

43. *VCM*, vv. 517–519. The resemblance of this passage with the first canto of the *Divine Comedy* will have been noted. The poet, wandering in the savage forest (*selva selvaggia*), is unable to leave because of a panther, a lion, and a wolf. [This prayer of praise lends itself to Christian use almost without change, at least for those who see not only the man Jesus Christ but also see *through* Jesus Christ to the Logos, understanding that the Reality of Jesus Christ the incarnate Son of God is precisely the Logos—and that the Reality of the Logos is *essential* Identity with the Father. TRS]

5

'WHO AM I?'

'WHO AM I?' When God manifested Himself to Moses in the Bush at Horeb, Moses addressed this question to Him: 'Who am I, that I should go to go to Pharaoh?'[1] The request for the Divine Name follows immediately, [2] as if to suggest a mysterious link between the identity of the man and the identity of God. It is as if the living Word of the Father, His Verb,[3] by which He perfectly and totally reveals His own identity ('He that seeth me seeth the Father also'),[4] was a challenge to the false identities of the man. To Moses' 'Who am I?' comes the divine response, 'I will be—or I am (Ehyeh) with thee.' This is already Emmanuel, and generally the Fathers have seen in the episode of the 'Burning Bush' a personal manifestation of the Word. Those Hindu masters who know the Bible attach a capital importance to this passage. Ramana Maharshi loved to say 'I am that I am' was the only phrase printed in capitals in the Bible.

The reader who has had the patience to follow us to this point will have noted the consistency with which we have resisted any notion of an identity *sensu composito* between God and man, which would merely be pantheistic monism, instead making of it a kind of divine and Trinitarian privilege, may perhaps ask himself: What have I,

1. Exod. 3:11.
2. Exod. 3:13.
3. The French language wisely uses two terms to convey the sense of the Second Person of the Trinity instead of the single term 'Word', as in English. The first of these terms, *Parole*, means Word or speech; and the second, *Verbe*, is cognate with its English counterpart, but carries a more eminently active sense than does the word *Parole*. Hence we translate the word *Verbe* by its nearest English equivalent, Verb. TRS
4. John 14:9.

myself, to do with such an identity? How does it concern *me?* This is a question which we must now try to answer, but without concealing that, at first glance, this response will necessarily be disappointing and a little ambiguous.

We have used the word 'antinomy' on several occasions. For centuries, supporters and opponents of non-dualism have argued back and forth, the latter denouncing the incoherences of a doctrine which the former attempt to present in an ordered and logical manner, though without being able to achieve this completely, because it is in fact, impossible. In verse 109 of the *Vivekacudamani,* Shankara consequently introduces the concept of *Māyā,* 'cosmic illusion', which, as we have seen, is also 'divine Power'.

> It cannot be said of Her that She exists or that She does not exist, nor that She participates simultaneously in existence and non-existence. She is neither homogenous nor heterogeneous, nor at once both the one and the other. She is neither composed of parts nor entirely indivisible, nor both the one and the other. *Māyā, the Great Wonder, eludes all description.*

We note the analogy between this notion of *Māyā* and the Scholastic notion of *materia prima,* an analogy that is only partial, however, for *Māyā* is also—and for Shankara, even primarily—the *potentia activa* (active power) to which we alluded when we spoke of creation, and which is not really distinguished from the divine Essence since it is the very Power (*Shakti*) of the Lord, according to Shankara.[5]

We should not be deceived by the apparent clarity of our exposition. It would be seriously misleading to imagine that, at least as to the essentials, we can form a perfectly complete and adequate idea of Indian non-dualism, as if the latter simply taught the illusory character of the world and nothing more, which would involve no

---

5. Cf. René Guénon, *L'Homme et son Devenir,* p 92, n 1:
This is why *Brahma* Itself is *Purushottama,* while, with regard to manifestation, *Prakriti* only represents Its *Shakti,* that is to say, Its 'Productive Will', which strictly speaking, is 'omnipotence' ('non-acting' activity with regard to the Principle, becoming passivity with regard to manifestation); see also *idem,* p 54, 'According to the *Purānas,* it (*Mūla-Prakriti,* 'primordial Nature') is identified with *Māyā,* conceived as 'mother of forms'....

apparent contradiction and perhaps no problem. If we held this position, the no less essential *antinomic aspect* of Vedantic teaching, which until now we have only touched on, would be completely lacking. We can formulate this as follows: *there is not, there has never been, and there will never be, anyone suffering illusion.* Let us again quote Shankara:

> *Māyā* gives rise to both bondage and liberation, but in the Self (*Ātmā*) these exist no more than the serpent which, appearing and disappearing by turns, exists in the rope whose nature has never changed. Bondage and liberation: it would be permissible to use these terms if one could ascertain the presence or absence of a mask that would hide the Real, but as regards *Brahma* can such a mask exist? *By what could Brahma be hidden since nothing other than Brahma exists?*[6]

Thus what is implied in the frequently reiterated assertion that Deliverance is not the production of a non-preexisting result, now appears in all clarity. Suddenly losing his footing and about to founder, man anxiously asks himself: But then, WHO am I? What, therefore, is this I?—which question, from an Eastern perspective, is the beginning of all wisdom. Even more than from Hamlet's perspective, we should say: THAT is the question! But this question, which the Orient never ceases to ask, seems of no concern to Western man, at least until the last few decades, although of late upheavals have begun to change that.

> It is the history of each one of us over the course of these recent years. We have been brought violently back to ourselves, as if shaken by an earthquake, the violence of the storm abruptly stripping us of all conceptual artifices which have clothed us and formed our bonds.[7]

Until recently Western man seemed never to have been touched by the suspicion that in reality he might be something other than he

6. VCM, vv. 569–570.

7. Régis Jolivet, *Les Doctrines existentialistes de Kierkegaard à J.P. Sartre* (Paris: Éditions de Fontenelle, 1948), p 29.

appeared. He seemed not to have felt the need to question himself. If he still happened to remember the ancient exhortation, 'Know thyself!'[8] it was always to see therein a simple invitation to continue in the direction and on the plane of what he *knew* about himself once and for all, without a return to essentials. He could conjugate his 'identity' without hesitation and with perfect assurance: he was so-and-so, son of so-and-so, born at such a time, in such a place, having such qualities and such faults, corporeal or spiritual. It was only here and there that isolated mystics, under the intrusion of an unwonted Light and Strength, begin to doubt the claims of the secular state to express their real being in an adequate and exhaustive manner. Here we should quote a remarkable intuition of Leon Bloy:

> It is the most common of illusions to believe that one is really what one seems to be, and this universal illusion is corroborated throughout life by an ongoing deception of all our faculties. Nothing less than death is necessary to teach us that we are always deceived. At the moment our identity (which is so completely unknown to us) is revealed, inconceivable abysses will be uncovered before our *true* eyes—gaping depths both within and outside ourselves. Men, things, events will finally be exposed, and each one of us will be able to verify the assertion of this mystic, who says that since the Fall the entire human race has been in a deep sleep.[9]

And yet, is there anything in the whole world so truly crucial? Of what use is it to man to know the world if he is ignorant of himself? But it seems that several centuries of exclusively examining external things in an attempt to wrench from them their secrets have made Western man incapable of any truly interior and profound task. How, in these conditions, would he be capable of understanding the warning of the *Katha Upanishad*:

---

8. Cf. Pierre Courcelle, '*Connais-toi toi-même; de Socrate à saint Bernard*', *Études Augustiniennes*, Paris, 1974.

9. Cited in Jacques Maritain, *Approches sans entraves* (Paris: Fayard, 1973), pp 45–46.

The faculties of man are turned outward, and therefore he looks outward and not within himself towards the interior mystery. He who is wise, however, and desirous of immortality, turns his eyes within and beholds the Self.[10]

Let us allow ourselves to be introduced to this problem of the 'Quest for the Self', so alien to our mentality, by a man who, as very few before him, both experienced and accepted the urgency in its uncompromising purity, Ramana Maharshi:

Is the world real, or is it illusory?
Does it have a form, or is it formless?
Is it joyful, or is it sorrowful?
Without worrying about the world,
Be concerned first of all with yourself!
When you open your eyes,
Does not the world awaken for you?
When you close your eyes,
Does it not disappear?
When you think of it, it exists for you
When you sleep, where is it?
Therefore seek first who it is by whom the world exists for you.
Who is the Knowing, who is the unknowing;
He who knows, he who does not know.
What is knowledge of oneself? what is one's ignorance?
Knowledge of Whom? Ignorance of Whom?
Such is the real question.[11]

Before attempting a response, insofar as one might be possible on the level of words and concepts (it might be said that on the rational level, the essence, the signification, the very possibility of the *I-being* are an impenetrable enigma *because they consist of the very one who poses the question*), we must first of all carefully clarify a point of terminology which seems to us so much the more important because

---

10. *Katha Upanishad*, trans. Louis Renou (Paris: A. Maisonneuve: Bordeaux, impr. de Bière, 1943), IV, 1.

11. Ramana Maharshi, *Ulladu-Nārpadu* [*Forty Verses on Reality*. No bibliographic information given by the author].

of the imprecision reigning in this subject among those authors who are too often responsible for planting in the reader's mind the very confusions regarding the true nature of the being which the non-dualist doctrine is supposed to dispel. The pantheist confusion is one of these, but it is not the only one.

On several occasions already we have drawn attention to the error of translating *Ātmā* by 'soul'. Assuredly, the sense of the word 'soul' can be expanded to express new concepts, and in some measure common usage must be taken into account if we are to avoid being misunderstood. It is a fact that when a Westerner utters the word 'soul', whether or not he believes in the existence of such an entity, he generally has in mind a rather precise notion, one which has almost nothing in common with the Vedantic notion of *Ātmā*, as will be seen much better in what follows. We believe that the word that renders this idea least inadequately remains 'Self'.[12] Certainly it is not perfect, but at least it has the advantage of being unrelated grammatically to any determined subject, and it is this consideration which leads us to adopt it. For the opposite reason we prefer to avoid the word 'I' which, even capitalized, spontaneously evokes the idea of a particular being who by his very existence implies the existence (and the exclusion) of other similar 'I's', multiple and similarly limited. Its use in the context of non-dualism, inevitably suggests—especially to the Westerner—the specifically pantheistic idea of pure identity between the creature as such and the Creator. Even less could we think of using neologisms such as 'super-ego' expressly invented to translate concepts alien to those with which we are presently concerned, which pertain to other disciplines, and which are manifestly lacking any 'super-natural' character. As for the word 'I', it is quite difficult if not impossible to avoid its use entirely, even if only in the question 'Who am I?' But we must always be careful to specify, as we did in the second chapter for the formula 'I am *Brahma*', just which is the 'I' of which we speak. In the Vedic mantras the 'I' is not this identity formed by

12. In Sanskrit, the word *atman* takes the place of the reflexive pronoun 'Itself'. Cf. René Guénon, *Man and His Becoming according to the Vedānta* [chap. 2, p25, in the English language edition of Sophia Perennis, 2001, TRS].

birth and concealing the Self like a theatrical mask, as we shall see further on, even though it is the only thing which we naturally and therefore *fatally* perceive of ourselves.

Let us return to the question put before the reader at the beginning of this chapter: what have I, *myself*, to do with such an identity? How does it concern me? If by 'I' is meant the 'human person' in the sense in which this is understood in the West, that is, to the *individual* formed by the union of soul and body and falsely identified as the *person*—in brief, if we speak of the *ego*, or rather, if it is the *ego* which speaks of itself (and this is so because only the *ego* asks questions), then the response must be that *I* have nothing to do with such an identity which in no way concerns me. Let us say once again that the analogy between the created *esse* and the uncreated *Esse* approaches the equivocal character of an infinitesimal 'quantity', suggesting the image of an 'unreal' reflection. *It is the semblance of a surface on a depth of quasi-total otherness. Quis ut Deus!* [Who is like God?]. *Being* is not of a nature in which uncreated *Being* and created *being* could be two species. There is nothing common between the one and the other except this tenuous analogy without which there would be no occasion to speak of 'creature' because then *there would be nothing at all,* as we saw in the last chapter.

We have just said that the individual is falsely identified with the person. From a Thomist perspective, we have in fact refrained from confounding *individuation*, that is to say a simple effect of 'quantified matter' (*materia signata quantitate*) and the true person. 'Individual' is said in relation to the species, 'person' in reference to God. The one pertains entirely to the 'horizontal' order without in any way going beyond it, the other to the 'vertical' order. Regarding St Thomas' notion of individuality, permit us to cite Fr Rousselot:

It is necessary to say why the saints in the supernatural state of grace or the state of celestial beatitude do not behave as independent beings exterior to one another, seeming rather to have

returned to the apparently inferior state of substantial conditioning and intimate union belonging to members of the same
body. St Thomas' response to the question was his theory of
individuality, which can be considered a critique of the notion of
'complete individuality'. He destroyed the illusion of the self-
contained individual, and showed that egoism in its restrictive
form is not a truly natural inclination. . . . If we recall St Thomas'
ideas on human individuality and the restrictions which material potentiality entails for its development as an intelligent
being, we will understand that he [St Thomas] found no difficulty in adopting as his own the ascetic doctrine of a St Bernard.
Individuality must be sacrificed insofar as it is restrictive and
stubbornly clings to the animal illusion of a particular good; but
to sacrifice its limits is to gain an advantage, because the soul is
intelligent, that is to say, the potentiality of all.[13]

The *ego* is first of all a 'creature', that is, a semblance of *being*, an
expression and projection of true Being, a reflection whose entire
reality must be sought outside of and beyond its own limits, its own
finitude, which is to say that the creature is not its *own* reality. But
this is only the definition of what is created in general. How do we
define the *ego* as such? Let it be understood: in no way is this a question of a philosophical definition. What is it *to our interior eye*, when
we consider it *from within*? Shankara is about to tell us.

   'Engendered by the Self, the sense of the ego masks the Reality of
the Self. It appears all alone in the field of consciousness *as if it owed
its existence to itself.*[14] Here is the key: *the ego is the illusion of aseity.*
It is this and nothing but this. This is its entire essence. When the
illusion of aseity disappears, the sense of the *ego, which is this very
illusion,* disappears with it. And thus it is clearly seen that in reality
there never was and will never be any deluded one, *because the ego is
at once both the one deluded and the illusion.* Let us again say that it is
not a question of a philosophical definition, and in no way do we

   13. Pierre Rousselot, *Pour l'histoire du problême de l'amour au moyen âge* (Paris:
Vrin, 1933), pp31–32, 57.
   14. *VCM*, v. 142.

situate ourself on the level of concepts. In theory, the idea we form for ourselves of the 'human person' can quite easily exclude aseity (and it is necessarily so for Christians); but it is no less true that the *experience* that I have within myself of the 'I' as 'person' is an *experience of aseity,* and, again, that this experience *is* the ego and therefore it cannot but be illusory, *insofar as we spontaneously attribute to aseity the nature of the ego,* as we shall say below. In this connection Jacques Maritain speaks of a 'lived contradiction' and of an 'incompatibility of fact'. And here we must quote this important passage despite its length:

> *How can it be that I am born?* It is when a man is engaged in a purely intellectual act of thought (insofar as this is possible for a reasoning animal), that the following intuition is produced: how is it possible that what is in the process of thinking, in the act of intelligence, that what is immersed in the fire of knowing and in the intellectual seizure of that which is, at one time was pure nothing, at one time did not exist? Here, where I am now in an act of intellection and consciousness of my thought, was once *nothing?* It is impossible, it is not possible that at a certain moment that which now thinks might not have been at all, might have been a pure nothing. How could this be born into existence? I am not confronting a logical contradiction here, I am confronting a lived contradiction, an incompatibility of fact (known in *actu exercito*). It is as if I found myself in a room without having left it for an instant, and I am told that I have just entered it. I know that what is said to me is impossible. Thus the I who is now in the act of thinking always existed. This view imposes itself upon me and does not seem bizarre unless I withdraw to consider it from the outside.... But I know that I have been born. After all, I know it by hearsay; in the final analysis I know it with an absolute certitude, and moreover I remember myself from my childhood. It is this certitude of being born, common to all men, which suppresses in us the blossoming— when the natural spirituality of the intelligence is activated in us—of the other certitude, that of the impossibility that our existence as thinking minds may have had a beginning, or, of

itself, followed upon nothingness, and which prevents this latter certitude from becoming conscious. Here I am, caught between two contrary certitudes. There is only one solution: I have always existed, this I who thinks; but not in myself, not in the limits of my own personality, nor in an impersonal life or existence (without personality, no thought, and yet the thought was necessarily there because it is now in me), and therefore in a supra-personal existence or life. Where, then? It must have been in a being of transcendent personality, in whom was found supereminently all that there is of perfection in my thought and in all thought, and who in his own infinite self was, before ever I was, and who, now that I am, is more myself than I am myself, and who is eternal, and from whom the I which now thinks proceeded into temporal existence. I had (but without saying I) an eternal existence in God before receiving a temporal existence in my own nature and in my own personality.[15]

To dream that the ego could ever be liberated from illusion is therefore a deception because the ego is itself an illusion. This is why this illusion is described as 'without beginning or end'.[16] Once again, the essentially 'supra-natural' character of Deliverance is indicated, but this time in returning to the principle (we have already cited the verse which follows): 'Nothing can cut these bonds but the marvelous sword of Knowledge forged by discrimination, *when its edge has been sharpened by divine Grace.*'[17]

As we wrote above concerning the Supreme Identity, such an 'identity' does not concern *me*. In the face of such a declaration so bold as to seem forbidding, the reader will no doubt have felt some sense of incoherence. Now he may see the internal logic of it. Having no truth, the *ego* lacks identity. There is no other way to reach the true Self than simply to reject this borrowed character. 'Imitate the actor who, at the end of the last act, rejects the mask of the character he has just represented.'[18] 'Discrimination' (*viveka*) must bloom

---

15. Jacques Maritain, *Approches de Dieu* (Paris: Alsatia, 1953), pp 83–86.
16. *VCM*, v.146.
17. *VCM*, v.147.

into absolute 'renunciation' (*vairagya*). The *ego* is what must be denied. 'I know not the man.'[19] A so-called discrimination of the Real from the unreal that is incapable of culminating in rejection of the unreal can be only an illusion.

> Know, O wise disciple, that renunciation and discrimination are for man what wings are for the bird. Where one of these virtues is lacking, none aided by one alone can attain that climbing plant of Liberation, the flower of which blooms only at the pinnacle of the highest edifices.[20]

And in order that no one risk misunderstanding the purely interior and spiritual character of this renunciation of the *ego*, Shankara is careful to specify that

> deliverance does not consist in abandoning the gross body as the itinerant *sannyasin* abandons his staff or his bowl, but in rooting out all attachment from within himself, for attachment and ignorance are one.[21]

In order to outline the doctrine of cosmic Illusion we have until now made use of two images: the shimmering of the sun on the water, and the rope which a man takes for a serpent. Both, however, exhibit the same serious disadvantage, that the observer, an important element of the real, is exterior to the symbol. We will thus have to

18. *VCM* v.292. In this context we might recall that the Latin *persona*, from *personare*, originally designated the comedian's mask. [The words of Christ are pertinent here: *If any man would come after me, let him deny himself.* Matt. 16:24. TRS].

19. Matt. 26:72.

20. *VCM*, v.374.

21. *VCM*, v.558. This idea is familiar to Shankara who elsewhere writes: 'He who has renounced all, that man, O my friend, knows all' (*La 'Prashna' Upanishad et son commentaire par Shankarāchācharya*, translated from the Sanskrit and annotated by René Allar, in *Études Traditionnelles*, 1961, p291). The sentence from St John of the Cross, 'If you would become everything, strive to become nothing in nothing,' is comparable. (*La Montée du Carmel*, I, XIII, *Oeuvres spirituelles*, trans. Fr Grégoire de Saint-Joseph (Paris: Seuil, 1947), p86.

resort to a new image which eliminates this disadvantage, that of the man who dreams. But before examining it, let us first consider an intermediate image which, because it underscores the reversal of perspective that is involved, will allow us to interpret it correctly. We borrow this from Swami Ramdas, with whom it probably originates.[22] Ramdas is a *bhakta* and we should recognize that his philosophical judgments are sometimes open to question. The following statement is very characteristic of his manner: 'The aphorism 'the I is *māyā* and the not-I is *Brahman*' is excellent.'[23] Whatever can furnish a rule for practical action is excellent in his eyes, but from the purely speculative point of view it is simply of no interest.

What is in question is the relationship between two men, one of whom is 'liberated while living' (*jivan-mukta*) and the other not. *A priori* we might think that every interpersonal relation has ceased for anyone who has realized his identity with *Brahma* and who thereby has reintegrated in Himself everything which, from outside this point of view, appears as exterior or foreign. And no doubt this is so. But in a perspective such as that of Ramdas, who is a *bhakta*, it is precisely the interpersonal *relations* which express, insofar as this is possible, the absolute *non-dualism* of the Supreme Self.[24] Whatever one may think of the interpretation just offered—which, if we consider the essential rôle played by love, seems to us to render quite well the *raison d'être* and the function of the *bhaktic* 'way'—the following is Ramdas' solution: no doubt the Delivered makes no distinction between 'himself' and 'others', since in every being He sees Himself (here let us recall that 'the Delivered' *is a Name of Brahma*). In this respect he can be compared to a man looking at his own image in a mirror. *He distinctly sees two different forms, his own and its reflection, but he knows that the two forms are really only one.* In

---

22. Ramadasa, *Présence de Râm*, French translation by Jean Herbert of *The Divine Life* (Paris: Albin Michel, 1956), p91. [The author seems to conflate Ramadasa, b. 1608, author of *The Divine Life*, with Swami Ramdas, 1884–1963, author of *In Quest of God*. TRS]

23. Ibid., p59.

24. Cf. Epistle of St John, 4:12: 'No man hath seen God at any time. If we love one another, God abideth in us, and his charity is perfected in us.'

other words, the Delivered *sees* that the 'produced beings' have no
other reality than that which is communicated by Himself, which,
while being an exact expression of the doctrine of cosmic Illusion,
could also be an unexpected but faithful interpretation of the Judeo-
Christian doctrine of creation *ex-nihilo*, of which one also finds the
analog in Islam:

> God (*al-Haqq*) wished to see the essences (*a'yān*) of His most
> perfect Names, the number of which cannot be exhausted . . . in
> an all encompassing object which, being endowed with exist-
> ence, epitomizes the entire divine order thereby manifesting His
> mystery to Himself. For the vision that a being has of itself in
> itself is not the same as that provided by another reality which
> serves it as a mirror. There it manifests itself in the form deter-
> mined by the 'place' of the vision; the latter would not exist with-
> out the 'plane of reflection' and the ray that is reflected therein.[25]

Here we see that the observer is integrated into the symbol in which
he now holds the place, not of the reflection, *but of the real object.* A
true 'reversal of perspectives' is thus produced, and henceforth the
'point of view' is that of God-the-Producer of beings (*Brahmā* or
Ishvara) knowing these beings 'in themselves' (and not in Himself),
as His reflection in a mirror, that is to say, as so many 'projections'
and 'expressions' of Himself. And at this point we may note that if
we wished to understand the Gospel term 'parable' in its double
sense of 'figurative expression' and of (extra-divine) projection, the
word of the Lord concerning 'those outside' to whom 'everything
comes in parables' could express the relationship of the 'world' to
the 'mystery of the Kingdom"; existence 'far from the Lord' is like a
'parable' of the eschatological Kingdom, and the entire creation like
the 'place of parables'.[26]

In reality, as we have already had occasion to note, it is not in
their apparent exteriority that God knows His productions, but
in His Essence, in His Word, in their uncreated and eternal Truth.
The symbol of the dreamer should be interpreted from this last

25. Ibn 'Arabi, *Sagesse des Prophètes*, pp19–20.
26. Cf. Mark 4:11.

perspective. Just as the forms that appear in sleep, whether those with which one identifies oneself or those in which other individuals seem to play a role, are not other than the mental forms of the sleeper himself made from the [psychic] 'substance' of his mind (of course, the symbol of the spider weaving its web 'of its own substance' has the same meaning), so, analogically, all is equally 'God', all is equally 'the Self' for the one who sees things from this point of view, whether he may have effectively attained it or whether he places himself therein by 'faith'. This is a 'pan-theist' point of view, if one likes, but one which nevertheless does not confuse the 'created' and the 'uncreated' (or illusion and Truth) *since, by hypothesis, the created as such is excluded from its perspective.* It embraces no less the totality of the Real, being the point of view of God, shoreless Ocean of Being,[27] unique Source of universal existence to Whom nothing can be added from the exterior which He does not already contain within Himself. In truth one cannot see why, in principle, a legitimate use of the word 'pantheism' should not be possible. Did not St Paul himself write: ινα ή θεος τά πανατα έν πασιν [that God may be all in all].[28] But in fact this term has become identified with the systems it has served to designate and which are naturally unacceptable, not only for the Christian faith but even philosophically. And then, there is the *odium theologicum*...

We have just said that this point of view does not confuse Truth and illusion. This is quite accurate insofar as the 'illusory being' is identified purely and simply with the 'created being', but this identification calls for one reservation. We have already noted that from the perspective of non-dualism, even the degree of pure Being (*Ishvara*) remains 'illusory' in that this is the degree of 'principial manifestation', and this is why it can be symbolized by a sleeping man. However, it is not strictly a question of illusion unless he who dreams is unaware that he dreams. The symbol of the dreaming

---

27. 'For It is He who gathers in Himself the totality of Being like an ocean of *ousia*, without limits and without shores,' St Gregory Nazianzus, Sermon 45, *In sanctum Pascha*, III; repeated by St John Damascene, *De fide orthodoxa, I-1,* IX, in J.-P. Migne, *Patrologia Græca,* vol. 94, co.l 833.

28. I Cor. 15:28.

man therefore admits a double interpretation. In the case of the sleeper not conscious of dreaming, we have an image of cosmic Illusion properly speaking, that is to say, of that misunderstanding by which the being (and despite the profoundly enigmatic character of such an assertion, we are obliged to say that this 'being' is the ego), then appears to have dealings with other similar egos exterior to and distinct from himself, since he imputes the nature of the ego to the Self, just as the sleeper identifies himself with only one of the mental forms of his dream to the exclusion of others. In reality, the true Self is total Reality, Infinite, and outside of which there is nothing, or rather, of which there is neither outside nor inside. Now the sleeper who is conscious that he dreams cannot properly be said to be 'deluded'. He is in the situation of the man who looks at his image in a mirror knowing that the image is 'he', with the difference that here the 'forms' that are viewed, instead of being exterior and sensible (which would be represented by extra-divine created existences), are interior and mental (which represent the archetypes of beings *in divinis*). But if the sleeper who is conscious of dreaming cannot properly be said to be 'deluded', if he realizes the unity and the identity of the forms of the dream both as between themselves and in relation to him, the dreamer, he nevertheless remains asleep, that is, 'immersed' in a world which he himself produces. It is only when he is fully awake that the images dissipate and only the pure Self remains, free, unconditioned, unlimited, as in reality it has always been. All distinctions will then be extinguished. For Him, henceforth identified with the Supreme (*Parabrahma*), there will be neither 'outside' nor 'inside', neither 'Producer' (*Brahmā*), nor 'produced', neither 'Creator' nor 'creatures', neither 'Truth' nor 'illusion', neither 'Liberation' nor 'servitude', *under their aspects of distinct realities*, but only THAT, the Supreme, totally unlimited. *Tat tvam asi*, 'Thou art That'.

This state of *Ātmā* (which is not other than *Ātmā* Itself) beyond all limitative conditions whatsoever, and which we have symbolized here by the man who is fully awake, is sometimes symbolized in Hinduism by deep and dreamless sleep (*prajñā*). The analogy then rests on two points: the disappearance of all forms (symbolizing emancipation from all limits), and the extinction of the sense of the *ego* (which follows upon the first). But this is still only an image and it is plainly asserted that the Self is beyond the distinction of the three states of waking, dream, and deep sleep. This is why it is sometimes designated simply as the 'Fourth' (*Turiya*). 'I no longer have any more relation with the body than the ether has with a passing cloud. How can the states of waking, dream, and deep sleep, *these attributes of the body* touch me'?[29]

We can now see what the exterior observer corresponds to in the symbols of the sun on the water and the rope taken for a serpent. He was this 'illusory being' serving as the impossible junction of the Real and the unreal (of the sun and its reflection, of the rope and the appearance of a serpent) by the fact that he regarded both the one and the other *from without.* He was the floating 'being' who identified himself now with the Real, now with the unreal, thus posing that fallacious equation which is the root of all pantheisms: '(In me) the unreal *is* the Real,' He was that impossible *ego,* a pseudo-aseity appearing between the 'world' and 'God' as their common *limit,* point of incidence of the uncreated Ray on the 'surface of the waters'. Entirely relative to the *ego* and arising from its 'point of view', 'God' and 'the world' are no less illusory insofar as they exclude and limit one another by their very opposition. How could they be 'real' *since the Real is identical to the Infinite: Satyam Jñānam Ānantam Brahma?*[30]

---

29. *VCM*, v.500.

30. The Supreme Principle is Truth, Knowledge, the Infinite; cf. penultimate paragraph of chap. 3, above. TRS

6

'I AM NOT THE CHRIST'

HAVING COME TO THE END OF OUR ANALYSES, are we now in a
position to answer the question posed at the beginning of the third
chapter: according to the doctrine of non-dualism, is the Supreme
Identity, that is to say the identity of *Ātmā* and *Brahma,* the same as
the hypostatic union of Christian theology? We can indeed respond,
and the response is indubitably negative. Let us recall briefly what
the hypostatic union is. The expression designates the union in
Jesus Christ, without mixture or confusion, of the divine and
human natures in the unity of the eternal Person of the Word, *in
such a way that everything accomplished or endured by the God-Man
is really and truly imputable to the divine Person itself.* This is and
must be considered fundamental, for responsibility and merit are
essential elements of all soteriology. If the acts (and the Passion) are
not *truly and personally* imputable to the only Son, co-eternal with
the Father, then there is no universal salvation, the Christ is not He
who saves, the Redeemer of all men and of man in his entirety, and
His name Jesus is a lie. In conformity with the very meaning of the
word 'hypostatic' in theology, we see that here *the central element is
the notion of person.* Now this is enough to make it quite clear that
what is involved is something entirely different from the Supreme
Identity of non-dualism. A decisive and very curious text enables us
to put a finger on it.

We borrow this delectable account from the teaching of
Ramakrishna. The protagonist, Vyāsa, is considered the creator of
Vedantic 'philosophy', as the codification of the *Brahma Sūtras* is
attributed to him. We cite the end of the account following the non-
dualist variation given in a note, as this version seems preferable to
us with regard to Vyāsa. At the moment when the sage Vyāsa was

about to cross the Jamuna River, the *gopis* (young women cow herders) arrived at the same spot, also seeking to cross over. Finding no ferry, they asked the advice of Vyāsa. He said to them:

> 'Do not worry, I will get you across the Jamuna, only I am very hungry; first give me something to eat.'The *gopis* offered him their provision of milk, cream, and fresh butter, and he ate it all. The *gopis* then asked: 'And now, how to cross over the river?' Vyāsa, standing on the bank, began to pray, 'Oh! Jamuna, if I have acquired virtue without eating anything today, grant us the power to cross thy bed with dry feet in order to get to the other side, and separate thy waters for this purpose.' He had hardly said these words when the waters of the river flowed back and the bed became dry. The stupefied gopis exclaimed, 'How can he say "I have eaten nothing today" when he has just eaten so much!' They did not understand that this was proof of the profound faith of Vyāsa. 'I have eaten nothing' signifies, 'I am the *Shuddha Atman*, the Pure Self, who is affected by nothing. . . .'[1]

It would be difficult to find a text more explicit or one that better shows, by illustrating in a manner as vivid as it is picturesque, the radical opposition that exists between the Christly mystery of the hypostatic union as it has always been understood by the unanimous tradition of the Church, and the Vedantic notion of the supreme Self identified with the Infinite, which Self, because of this identification, does not act, does not suffer, is not affected by anything, because there is nothing which is really exterior, It being the totally Real.

> I am without activity and without change, without parts and without form, absolute and eternal. I have no support other than myself. I am the One without a second. [2]

Fundamentally, and in spite of the conceptual reservations we have had to formulate as regards the 'doctrine' of Ramdas, his own vision of things is not so very different. Two passages from his *Carnet de*

---

1. Ramakrishna, *L'Enseignement*, no. 744.
2. VCM, v.515.

Pèlerinage taken together, seem to outline his thinking. In the first, responding to a friend who asserts that in him he sees Rām (that is to say, the Divinity), in person, he declares,

> In fact, Rām does not speak; the moment he speaks, he is no longer Ram. Words always presume a duality: he who speaks and he to whom one speaks. *Rām is one and indivisible. For the man for whom the ego is the principal obstacle to the Realization of the unity of God, it is pure ignorance to declare that he is God.*[3]

Having thus formally denied to man all divine identity *sensu composito*, Ramdas, in another passage of this same *Carnet*, goes on to assert non-dualism no less clearly, and in Shankarian terms. To a pious devotee who asked him if he would like something to eat, he responded,

> 'To whom do you ask this question?' 'To you', his interlocutor replies. Ramdas then asked, 'Does something exist which might be 'you' and 'me' when all is only one? Is not everything visible like a rope which one takes for a serpent, like the son of a barren woman, like the horns of a hare and like a flower. . . .' The other then interrupted him with, 'I see that you are at a higher stage', and left.[4]

In the juxtaposition of these texts from Ramdas we have a striking example of these 'changes of points of view' (the 'higher stage') so characteristic of oriental thought and so disconcerting to the Western observer. Here we find ourselves confronting an articulation of *bhaktic* doctrine and of Shankarian non-dualism; their imprint seems to have strongly marked the spirituality of Ramdas, *bhakta* by vocation and technique, who 'played at seeming to be different from Him.'[5]

The stupefaction and incomprehension of the *gopis* at the strange attitude of Vyāsa only translates *in vivo* what Shankara states in his

3. Ramdas, *Carnet de pèlerinage*, trans. Jean Herbert (Paris: Albin Michel, 1973), pp 64–65.

4. Ibid., p 203.

5. Ibid., p 9.

teaching, namely, that it is almost impossible for man to doubt his sentiment of being the author and owner of his acts. 'Even when he has already made the truth his own,' writes Shankara, 'man retains the powerful and indelible . . . impression that he is himself the agent (*kartā*) and the sensible subject (*bhōktā*).'[6]

From the first chapter we have drawn the reader's attention to the fact that the true Self, identical with *Brahma*, is not a nature, that it is without qualities, without attributes, actionless, 'For he who acts is other'; in brief, *that it is not a subject*—but perhaps the reader did not then perceive the full impact of these assertions. Now he can see clearly that in reality nothing is further removed from a *personal* union of the Divine and the human. In the case of the hypostatic union we are in the presence of a unique Being uniting in His Person the created and the uncreated in such a manner that, as we have said, it is truly and really the Divine Person who acts and suffers. In the case of the Supreme Identity it is the pure Self, 'this absolutely unconditioned Self, this Self who does not act,'[7] who is total Being (or rather total Reality beyond the distinction of Being and Non-Being), the Infinite without a second, and therefore without relationship with any otherness whatsoever (because there is no 'other'; and, moreover, no 'same'), because, once 'realized', there is neither relativity nor alterity, *and thereby, no person.* The hypostatic union is truly the union of *two* realities which, united in the Person of the Word, *wherein each retains its respective reality,* created or uncreated, the distinctions being preserved. The Supreme Identity *is not* a union but, as Ramdas said in one of the texts we cited, 'the Realization of the Unity of God', or more precisely still, of the Non-dualism of the Supreme, because situated beyond pure Being and coextensive with Metaphysical Unity and the principle of multiplicity, it mysteriously surpasses all duality (*dvanda*), *including even the Creator-creature duality itself.*

It is now quite clear that *the hypostatic union is not the Supreme Identity.* In this connection let us recall what we said in the first chapter, that there are degrees of unity just as there are degrees of

6. *VCM,* v.267.
7. Ibid., v.153.

identity, and we then applied the expression of supreme Unity to the Unity of the Trinity. We also said that God *is* Identity which ultimately amounts to the same thing. Thus the unity which in Christ constitutes the union of the divine and human natures (we do not speak here of the Unity of the Person *which is not constituted by this union*), even while being of a more elevated order than that of body and soul in the human composite, nevertheless constitutes an inferior degree of unity when compared to the supreme Unity of the Trinity.

The hypostatic union is thus not the Supreme Identity. This conclusion has considerable import for our subject. In order to accept the Vedantic doctrine of non-dualism, there is in fact no need for a hypothetical extension of the hypostatic union to the entire human race, even to all creatures, which would obviously be opposed to Christian faith. Another consequence of no less importance: the objection that we examined at length in the third chapter without finding a fully satisfactory solution, that God cannot be held *personally* responsible for the sin of man—rather embarrassing if the hypostatic union is extended to the entire human race[8]—is quite simply of no interest from the perspective of the Supreme Identity, *which is not a personal union.*

We spoke of extension of the hypostatic union to all creatures. We must not forget that the Supreme Self is the permanent Truth not only of man but of everything whatsoever that exists. Now as it seems to us, we cannot properly speak of hypostatic union, human or other, except for beings endowed with life and intelligence, that is to say, for beings who, in the absence of this union, would nonetheless have been created 'persons' in virtue of their nature. This remark further corroborates our conclusion that if the Supreme Self is the Truth of everything that exists, including animals without reason, vegetables, and even minerals, it is quite evident that the union

---

8. Cf. Heinrich Denzinger, *Enchiridion symbolorum: definitionum et declarationum de rebus fidei et morum,* [no publication information given TRS], n3816, condemning the 'panchristism' which amounts to attributing to man a divine character *and to Christ error and the inclination to evil:* 'Et dum hominibus divina attribuunt, Christum Dominum erroribus humanaeque in malum proclivitati obnoxium faciunt.'

(the creative union) of God and this stone, for example, however it may be conceived, cannot be said to be 'hypostatic'. God is not the 'person' of this stone, anymore than of this duck, of this willow, or of this dragonfly. A stone is not a 'divine person', even though the Creator is entirely present in his indivisible unity, by his 'presence of immensity'.

We have just written 'however it may be conceived,' for despite the real harmony that exists (as we hope has been demonstrated) between the Judeo-Christian concept of creation and the Hindu notion of 'divine manifestation', it remains true that the perspectives are quite different from each other, the distance separating the points of view naturally being expressed by a distortion of perspectives and a shift of planes, in the intellectual as well as the sensible orders. If from the Hindu perspective God cannot be said to be the 'person' of this stone or this rock, He is nevertheless their Truth. If a Hindu had used our categories of thought, he would probably say something like this: it is a personal God (*Īshvara*) who is the Creator of all being and of every being, including material beings. These latter, who are not 'persons', thus have nothing personal other than God who produced them and who, by His presence and providential action, sustains them in being from moment to moment. This is not to deny secondary causes, but these, because they are secondary and created, cannot be regarded in any way as *intermediaries* between the Creator and His creature to whom, at this very moment, He *directly and immediately* gives all that it has of being. The Creator God is totally present, without separation, in each of His creatures and in each part of them.[9] When the tiger pounces on its prey, even though it cannot be said to be the divine person, does not this *act*, like all that exists, have its *first* cause in God who permits it and without which it would not take place, as we noted in the third chapter when speaking of the divine 'concurrence'? 'Are not two sparrows sold for a farthing? and not one of them shall fall on the ground without your Father.'[10] In order to avoid the appearance of contradiction, let us note that what is involved here is not the

9. Cf. *Summa Theologica*, IaP, Q8, A3.
10. Matt. 10:29.

Supreme (*Parabrahma*) since the Infinite is 'non-acting' (on *what* would it act?), but the personal God (*Ishvara*) in his 'triple manifestation' (*trimūrti*) as Producer (*Brahmā*), Preserver (*Vishnu*), and Destroyer (*Shiva*) or, more precisely, 'Transformer' of beings. Nevertheless, it must not be thought that *Brahmā* is other than the Supreme. We have already noted that *Brahmā*, as such, is 'illusory'; *Brahmā* IS *Brahma*.

Perhaps it will be asked: cannot this Indian manner of conceiving the 'presence of immensity', that is to say, this intimate, immediate, and 'entifying' presence of the Creator to His creature, be compared to a kind of universal, 'natural' and permanent 'transubstantiation"? Does not the idea of a universe 'without reality' and of 'pure appearance' make one think of the Eucharistic species?[11] It cannot be doubted that there is in fact a valid analogy; however, we do not think that it could be pushed as far as identity. We said above that Deliverance must not be represented as a kind of 'transubstantiation' of the human into the Divine. If we now speak of a valid analogy, there is no contradiction. Indeed, our comparison revolves around the respective results of Deliverance and the Eucharistic consecration and, more especially, on the fact that the latter operates a change while the former does not. Here we compare the 'illusory' character of the created world with the similarly 'illusory' character of the Eucharistic species *after consecration*, which is quite different. The analogy is valid, but even so, it is very necessary to see the difference. The Eucharistic species no longer conceals any substance of bread or of wine (taking 'substance', of course, in the philosophical and not in the *chemical* sense of the term), while what is 'illusory' in the case of the created world, as we have frequently pointed out, is the real and *subsistent* creature. In order that comparisons of this kind may truly elucidate the question, it is always necessary to consider not only the point wherein the analogy lies, but also that or those where irreducible differences subsist, lacking which one runs the danger of simplifications and abusive generalizations. Perhaps it

---

11. In the *Osservatore Romano*, August 25, 1981 (weekly French edition), devoted to the Eucharist, Innos Biffi suggests the particularly happy term (as it seems to us) of 'trans-identification'.

might not be impossible, nevertheless, to find the beginning of a *rapprochement* between the two points of view in the distinction we have just set out between the philosophical and chemical points of view in which the word 'substance' might be understood. We submit the question to theologians.

What is quite essential and should be retained from these reflections is the clear distinction between hypostatic union and Supreme Identity, a distinction that does not close off all possibility of Christianity admitting the Hindu doctrine of non-dualism, with the necessary adaptations. Moreover it will have been made clear that the special problem in this regard is not so much the illusory character of the created world (we believe we have shown the compatibility with Christian teaching on creation *ex nihilo*), as the assertion of an identity, though profoundly mysterious, of man and the Infinite, understood in the sense of an Identity fully *actual in itself.* That is perhaps, after all, the reason why the 'Suggestions for Dialogue' of the Secretariat for Non-Christians preferred to speak of an 'ideal of identification with the Absolute.' We ourselves do not think that such an 'ideal', insofar as it might be something other than a pure chimera (as we have already indicated), would be any easier to admit, everything considered, than this actual and permanent identification taught by *Advaita Vedānta,* on condition that it be correctly understood. Indeed, we think it would be less so.

Another difficulty, no less serious, results from the idea of the 'non-personal' Infinite (we do not say *an* infinite), and consequently of the 'relatively relative' (if we may use such an expression) and 'illusory' character of the personal God Himself. Here too, however, and despite appearances, if a personal union understood *strictu sensu,* that is as the union of the human race with the Divinity *in the unity of a unique divine Person,* is excluded, the idea of the Identity of all being in the non-personal, or 'supra-personal', Infinite—transcendent and profoundly mysterious Identity, as we said—is not itself excluded. *On the contrary, its negation would contradict the idea of the Infinite as precisely that outside of which there is nothing.*

We can readily summarize all these difficulties in saying that everything, or nearly everything, revolves about the notion of *person.* How should we conceive it? What exactly should be understood by this word? As we said, how can we speak of identity where it is said that the person has disappeared? How can we envisage a 'relativity' of the person, how even admit it? These are the questions which we now wish to resolve more precisely and in the measure of our means, and insofar as the 'hard kernel' is not simply impenetrable to rational analysis. Moreover, we are aware that in what follows there are elements that will seem extraordinary to Western thought.

When in the fifth chapter we distinguished the true person from the *ego* understood as the soul-body composite which Western thought calls the 'human person', it might have been thought that a *nec plus ultra* had been reached and that it was not possible to progress further because there was nothing beyond. However, returning to our first image in which the Sun represents the 'Divine Personality' and its reflection the *ego*, we see that the Sun did not represent *all* Reality because it left something outside itself which made us then refer to it as 'quasi-absolute reality'. The 'person', however we conceive it, cannot be the last word concerning the Real. We have already had occasion to note that there is no 'person' where there is no *relation* and *otherness*. The idea of a *unique* person who could be identified with the totality of the Real, and that of a *personal* Infinite, are thus equally illusory; both amount to the same thing and differ only in the inversion of substantive and adjective. 'As Creator, God is both Trinity and Unity. As Infinite, He is neither Trinity nor Unity, nor anything that can be enunciated.'[12]

Further, we could in all strictness speak of an absolute 'I' by transposing the notion expressed by the *personal* pronoun in order to make it express, as far as possible, the Supreme Identity where all *relation* disappears—and in a sense, one is obliged to do this. But it seems to us that it would be difficult to speak of an *infinite* 'I'. But since there is no 'thou' except in reference to an 'I', we think it an

12. Nicolas of Cusa, *Œuvres choisies,* p 429 [no specific work given. TRS]

abuse of language to speak of the absolute 'Thou', as does the sentence we quoted in the second chapter.

'God', from the moment in which I conceive him as placed before me, or better and more exactly, from the moment wherein I conceive myself as *placed before Him,* that is to say where 'God' is considered as a being *in relation* to me, like a 'Thou' in relation to an 'I', is obviously no longer the Infinite outside of which there is nothing. He is rather one of the terms of a doubly reciprocal relation, a sort of refraction of the Infinite in the domain of duality which characterizes the finite and which, moreover, is 'illusory'. 'Many simple people', said Meister Eckhart, 'imagine that they must consider God over there and themselves here! This is not the way it is. God and I are one'.[13] The personal 'God' appears to *me* as a 'Thou' before an 'I', as if this 'I' had any existence of his own. In order to avoid all misunderstanding, we must emphasize that here we are not considering the *tripersonal* God of Christian revelation, but a *unipersonal* God appearing *before* a creature affirming itself as 'I'. Ramakrishna said plainly, 'As long as the "I" is found in me, the personal God is also found in me and reveals himself in glorious and various forms. . . .'[14] We must make it equally clear that this in no way implies that we need not pray to Him and adore Him; without the least doubt we must do so, because for as long as 'I' am, He is before me as the Face of the Absolute, *and it is He*—and not the Absolute, which would have no meaning—who will deliver me.

> If you want to know the Absolute [added Ramakrishna], invoke this *Brahman*[15] with attributes who hears your prayers, and it is He who will make you know the Absolute. *For He who is Brahman with attributes is also Brahman beyond attributes. Distinctions make for the perfection of knowledge.*[16]

13. Meister Eckhart, *Sermons,* vol. i, p86.

14. Ramakrishna, *L'Enseignment,* no. 1262.

15. *Brahman,* i.e., *Brahma,* the unqualified, the Supreme. See translator's footnote, chap ii, on the English language conventions governing the use of the terms.

16. Ibid., no. 1300. [Cf. John 14:6: 'No man cometh unto the Father but by Me.' TRS]

If it is said that we can always correct out conception of 'God', we readily acknowledge it, and this is precisely what we are doing. Nevertheless, it always remains *I* who corrects it, and therefore who continues to place *myself* before Him as an 'I', and sets Him before me as a 'Thou'. 'You cannot formulate Him as He is, because you must cover Him with an extraneous element which is your own personality.' [17] Ibn al-Arabi writes:

He [the believer] does not have knowledge [of God] but bases himself only on the opinion of which the divine word speaks: 'I conform Myself to the opinion that My servant has of Me,' which means 'I do not manifest Myself to my worshipper except under the form of his belief'.... The Divinity conformed to belief is that which can be defined, and That is the God which the heart can contain (according to the divine word: 'Neither My heavens, nor My earth can contain Me, but the heart of My faithful servant contains Me'), for the absolute Divinity cannot be contained by anything, since it is the very essence of things and His own essence. [18]

In these last words we perceive an echo of St Bernard's *qui suum ipsius est, et omnium esse.*

Identification with the Self (in the sense we have indicated, which is *to recognize oneself*, not to render oneself identical), would be impossible if there were not total 'dis-identification' with the 'I'. Or again, 'realization' of the Self (in the same sense of recognizing the Self as The Reality), would be impossible if there were not total 'de-realization' of the 'I' (and by way of consequence, of the 'Thou', since this latter is relative to 'me'). 'No one can see God without dying.' The word 'de-realization', however, calls for an explanation. For us it is in no way a synonym for reduction to nothingness or annihilation. We have often said that the idea of 'nothingness', that is, a nothingness substantiated, is only a pseudo-idea that answers to nothing real. Just as realization of the Self is not something other than what we have called being conscious (even though

17. Ibid., no. 1260.
18. Ibn 'Arabi, *Sagesse des Prophètes*, end of last chapter.

strictly speaking consciousness is simply a function of the 'I')—better rendered by the English word *awareness*—of one's permanent Reality, similarly the 'de-realization' of the 'I' is nothing but the awareness of one's permanent 'non-reality' *as 'I'*. *Therefore nothing is changed*. Not being the production of a non-preexisting result, Deliverance cannot be the restoration of something preexisting. In other words, that which truly *is* has always been and always will be, just as, conversely, that which has not always been and will not always be, truly *is* not. This is the formula of Gaudapadacharya whom we have already had occasion to quote. 'That which had no existence before and does not exist after does not exist now.' Such is the ego: a pseudo-aseity, the Reality of which is elsewhere.

We now ask the reader to be very attentive to what follows. When we speak of the *ego* as a pseudo-aseity, we do not wish to say thereby that there is no aseity. Quite to the contrary, we mean rather to assert the existence of a, or rather, *the* true aseity which is the 'very Self'. The entire illusion consists in this, that aseity is attributed to 'me', or, more accurately (for the preceding phrase is still sullied by the point of view of the *ego*), *the nature of the 'I' is attributed to aseity*. *All false imputation or superimposition aside, aseity is the pure Self*, which does not lie within the power of the *ego*—which latter is this very superimposition. As noted in the first chapter, this is the origin from which the indefinite sequence of existences (*samsāra*) *and notably this present link of the chain that is 'I'*, proceeds.

We cannot deal with the question of 'transmigration' here, but will simply say that this does not concern the 'human person'. 'The Lord is the only transmigrant.' 'The *jīva* [individual soul]', said Ramakrishna, 'is nothing but the incorporation (*embodiment*) of Satchitānanda,'[19] which excludes the possibility of such a thing as 'reincarnation of the soul'.[20] Genuine Masters generally try to turn their disciples away from this kind of consideration. To someone who seemed curious about his 'previous existences', Ramana Maharshi once responded, 'Ask rather if this time you are really

19. Ramakrishna, *The Gospel of Sri Ramakrishna*, trans. by Swami Nikhilananda (Madras: Sri Ramakrishna Math, 1974, 6th ed.), p101.
20. This equally excludes all theories of the 'pre-existence of the soul'.

born.'[21] As for Ramakrishna, when asked by a disciple, 'Do you believe in the reincarnation of the soul?' he gave the following answer, as astonishing as the question for those who think that 'Hindus believe in reincarnation':

Yes, they say there is something like that. How can we understand the ways of God with our small intelligences? Many have spoken of reincarnation; therefore I cannot disbelieve it.[22]

Three years later, asked again, 'Is there something such as reincarnation, are we born again?' he once more responded evasively:

Ask God. Pray sincerely to Him. He will tell you everything.... It is not good to seek to know these things at the beginning. Before all else, realize God, then He Himself will make you know everything which you wish.[23]

In reality, the reincarnationist illusion has its root in a confusion of the psychic and the spiritual. On the one hand it consists in confounding 'metempsychosis', understood in its true sense, which is to say the transmission of psychic elements, with a movement of the true being; and on the other, in falsely identifying 'transmigration', which is a passage of the being to a new state of existence defined by entirely different conditions, with a return to this our present world, which is a metaphysical impossibility. But this is enough on the question of reincarnation.[24]

In order to illustrate the doctrine of false imputation let us cite a text which, though not Hindu, expresses what we have said very clearly. The author is Mansur al-Hallaj. This will not be surprising if

---

21. Lakshman, *Étude* [no page given. TRS]
22. Ramakrishna, *Gospel*, p 84.
23. Ibid., p 903.
24. Guénon treated this important issue at length in *L'Erreur spirite* (English translation, *The Spiritist Fallacy*, Hillsdale, NY, Sophia Perennis, 2003). His essential point is that there can be no two identical possibilities, for if this were so, it would be a question not of two, but of a single, possibility; and 'God does not repeat Himsel.' Or, as Guénon wrote in *La Métaphysique orientale*, 'he who cannot step outside the point of view of temporal succession and envisage all things in simultaneous mode is incapable of the least conception of the metaphysical order.' TRS

it is recalled that in 'Suggestions for Dialogue', the Secretariat for Non-Christians compared the 'thou art That' of Hinduism with the 'I am the Real (God)' [*An al-Haqq*] of Hallajian 'mysticism'. Here is the passage which perfectly illustrates what we have said concerning the 'rejection of superimposed false imputations':

> I am 'I', and there are no more attributes; I am 'I', and there is no more qualification.... '*I' am the pure subject of the verb, no longer my self.* My actual 'I' is no longer myself. I am a metaphor (of God), not a generic likeness (to God), an apparition (of God), not a penetration (of God) in a material receptacle.[25]

In his study of Ramana Maharshi, Dr Sarma Lakshman wrote,

> I am quite simply 'I am', and all the rest is added to me by ignorance. This 'I am' is thus the element of truth in the ego. The false part of the ego is all that is added over and above, that is, the inconstant and always changing elements. This 'I am' is the only indication we have for finding the real Me.[26]

Leaving aside the mention of ignorance, this text is remarkably identical to that of al-Hallaj, who includes a very clear statement of the distinction between the hypostatic union and the Supreme Identity, to which our preceding analyses led us. In fact, it will have been noted that the terms used in the last sentence seem to have been chosen intentionally to avoid Christian ideas of 'consubstantiality' or of 'generation of the Word' ('not a generic likeness') and of 'Incarnation' ('not a penetration in a material receptacle'), which assuredly is nothing surprising on the part of a contemplative of Islam. This text is therefore precious both for its positive content and for the agreement that it attests to between the doctrines of al-Hallaj and the *Advaita* of Shankara.

Since we have alluded to the way in which Islam envisages Christ, it will not out of place to cite a 'perplexity' of Ibn al-Arabi whose

25. Louis Massignon, *Passion*, 521–522, in, *Opera Minora: texts recueillis, classes et présentés avec une bibliographie*, ed. Youakim Moubarac (Beirut: Dar Al-Maaref, 1963), v. 2, p401.

26. Sarma Lakshman, *Étude*, p89.

position in this regard seems to be, if not the closest to the Christian position, at least that which is least removed. 'All existences', he writes,

> are 'Words of God' which are never exhausted (Qur'an, XVIII, 109;[27] for all are only the word 'Be!' which is the Verb [Word] of God. Now, must it be believed that the Word is immediately attached to God in His principial state? If this is true it is impossible for us to know his quiddity; or rather does God 'descend' towards the form of the one who says 'Be', so that this word 'be' is the essential reality of the form towards which God 'descends', or in which He manifests Himself. Some knowers of God assert the first, others the second, and still others are in consternation at the ambiguity of the aspects. This question cannot be fathomed except by intuition. Abu Yazīd who breathed on the ant he had killed (inadvertently) and revived it, well knew by whom he breathed and that it was by Him that he breathed; his contemplation was Christic.[28]

If it is correct that he who says 'person' says 'relation', and that he who says 'relation' says 'relative', then it is false that the person might be that 'absolute' in which Westerners generally believe. Perhaps someone will object that at least in God, the Persons who are relations are nevertheless not relativized thereby. We would answer by saying that we must avoid confusing 'relative' and 'accidental'. It is precisely because the Father is *all-relative* to the Son that He is totally and uniquely Father; likewise, it is because the Son is *all-relative* to the Father that He is totally and uniquely Son. The mutual all-relativity of Son to Father and of Father to Son is the basis of their perfect equality: 'I and the Father are One.'[29] All the same, the Father, *Fons totius deitatis* [Fount of all Godhead], engenders; He is the Father and not the brother of His Son. The reciprocal relation

---

27. 'Say: If the sea were ink for the Words of my Lord, the sea would be spent before the Words of my Lord are spent, though we brought replenishment the like of it.' A. J. Arberry, *The Koran Interpreted* (London: Allen & Unwin, 1955), p 300.

28. Ibn 'Arabi, *Sagesse des Prophètes*, chapter on Jesus, p 117.

29. John 10:30.

uniting them, if one dare say it, is *sui generis*. While human paternity happens (*accidit*) to a being who was already something—a man—before being a father, the divine Paternity *is not added* (even from all eternity) to someone who was already something, to God, namely. By this, of course we do not wish to say that neither the Father nor the Son is God, but that no God exists outside the Father, the Son, and the Holy Spirit. There are in God three Persons and not four, and these three are only one God. Fundamentally, it is this *all reciprocal relativity* of the Son to the Father and of the Father to the Son that is signified in the words of St John: 'God is love.'[30] And we will add that, *being the Love for Another who is also Self* (but not personally), it is the only love that is not 'alienation'. The Father loves the Son, and the Son loves the Father, *as Himself.* This is the underlying reason that makes the second commandment really 'like unto the first.'[31] We can foresee the consequences of this doctrine for the subject occupying us here.

Thus, we repeat, whoever says 'person' says 'relation', and whoever says 'relation' says 'relative'. Moreover, since according to Vedantic doctrine the true Self is the Infinite, *that is to say, the essentially non-relative* (for all relativity assumes two terms), then, despite the profound obscurity of this assertion 'for me', we are led to say that *in relation to the [Supreme] Identity, the Person is still on this side, that it is something that must be surpassed in order to find the [Supreme] Identity.* Let us note that this is exactly the reverse of that 'depersonalization' which so many of our contemporaries look upon as an ideal. This latter is a disintegration, a dissolution, a reduction of the 'spirit' to 'matter' and to the 'mechanical'. The former is all embracing totalization, instantaneous, endless, without parts or boundaries—and also nameless (and here, too, this is the opposite of the 'anonymity' of the depersonalized masses), because 'silence is the veritable language of the true Self'.

In order to complete our examination of the relationship or of the lack thereof between the hypostatic union and the Supreme Identity,

30. I John 4:8 AV.
31. Cf. Matt. 22:39.

we have one last point to examine, but it is so unusual and delicate that we can hardly do more than mention it briefly. We now know that hypostatic union and Supreme Identity are two distinct notions which are even opposed in certain respects, but the question of their compatibility remains. Can a doctrine which posits the one as real admit the reality of the other? If the response to this question is affirmative, then we will have to ask what is the relation uniting them.

We begin by positing that the singular character of the hypostatic union agrees perfectly with the singularity of the mission and work of the divine Word, or, if preferred, with the vocation of the Messiah of God. This mission and this work being personal and strictly his own, it seems normal that the mode of divine union adapted to this mission and this work be similarly personal. It goes without saying that if we qualify the work of the Word as 'unique', this is not to deny the universal and catholic character of the salvation which it is His mission to bring and offer to all men; rather it is to signify, on the one hand, the singularity of the *event* of His advent among us, and, on the other hand, to mark that the sacrifice of the Word (a Hindu would say the sacrifice of *Purusha*) is the unique source of salvation, whose channels do not always necessarily follow paths familiar to us.[32] *The uniqueness of which we speak is the condition of universality. It is like the seal of the divine Uniqueness.*

32. Cf. René Guénon, 'À propos de quelques symboles hermético-religieux', *Regnabit*, December 1925: 'In other studies we hope to be able to show not only that the Center of the world is in fact identified with the Heart of Christ, but that this identification may have been clearly indicated in the doctrines of antiquity. Obviously in this case the expression 'Heart of Christ' should be understood in a sense which is not precisely what we might call 'historical', but, again, it must be said that historical facts themselves, like all the rest, convey higher realities according to their own modality, and conform to that law of correspondence to which we have alluded, a law which alone permits the explanation of certain 'prefigurations'. What is in question is the Christ-principle, that is, of the Word manifested at the central point of the universe. But who would dare claim that the eternal Word and his historical, terrestrial, and temporal manifestation are not really one and the same Christ under different aspects? Here again we touch on the relations between the temporal and the timeless; perhaps it is just as well not to dwell further on this, for these things are in fact among those of which symbolism alone permits the expression in the measure in which they can be expressed.'

In contrast, the Supreme Identity is characterized immediately and unreservedly by a universality that has, so to say, a more radical or principial significance. It is not limited to a single man, at once divine and human—Jesus—nor even to the whole of humanity, past, present, and future, but embraces the totality of existing things, that is to say, everything which to one degree or another participates in Being. It is and it remains for all times and for all conditions of existence, the immutable and transcendent Truth of everything that appears and disappears in an unending round of perpetual becoming. At once their Principle and their End, it is equally their veritable and ever present Reality since, we repeat, the very reality of the 'illusion' is 'illusory', although when it is considered from the point of view of beings such as we ourselves are in our present condition, it appears principally as our End and that of our fellow beings.

Let us summarize. We have on the one hand the hypostatic union or Incarnation of the divine Word, an *event* proper to a unique being. That union has its point of departure in time and, St Thomas tells us, is therefore something *created*.[33] On the other hand, we have the Supreme Identity, which is not an event or a fact, but the permanent and immutable Truth (and so *uncreated*), of all that exists. Thus, since they do not pertain to the same order of Reality, hypostatic union and Supreme Identity do not in themselves exclude one another, or stated otherwise, they are not metaphysically incompatible. Assuming that both are real, the question remains: what order links them together, because all that is real must be integrated in one way or another into the universal order.

As Christians we believe and confess that the Incarnation of the Word and His death on the Cross are truly and really the *center* and *pivot* of human and cosmic history, and that they establish—or re-establish—the bond between the world and man, on the one hand, and the transcendent and immutable Truth of God, on the other, a bond which had been sundered by the sin of Adam. This much is a

---

33. *Summa Theologica* IIIaP, Q2, A7, *sed contra: Omne quod incipit ex tempore est creatum. Sed unio illa ab aeterno non fuit, sed incepit ex tempore. Ergo unio illa est aliquid creatum.* (Everything that has a beginning in time is created. But this union was not from all eternity, but began in time. Therefore this union is something created.)

given, and it being acknowledged that the Supreme Identity is the universal End, it is permissible to hypothesize that the hypostatic union, that is, the redemptive Incarnation of the Word, be the *condition* and the *means* of His realization (in the sense in which we said that Deliverance by degrees should be understood), a realization which, for the Humanity of Christ, is effected by His death on the Cross, if we accept the interpretation of the *lamma sabacthani* given in chapter two. It is therefore by his *incorporation* in Christ and his participation in the Paschal mystery that man would receive the *possibility* of verifying the Supreme Identity in his person. The words of John Paul II quoted in the first chapter, '[Man] must, so to speak, enter into Christ with all his being, he must "appropriate" to himself and assimilate all the reality of the Incarnation and Redemption *in order to find himself*,' can be interpreted in this sense.

To this point we have considered the hypostatic union especially from the perspective that distinguishes it from every other mode of man's union with the Divinity, which is the most common theological perspective; in other words, we have envisaged it from the point of view of man. It remains for us to consider it from the point of view of God. The interest and the importance of this reversal of perspectives for our subject is clear, and what we have said concerning the various points of view from which the Real can be envisaged, and the consequences of passing from one point of view to the other, will once again be illustrated. Just as creation does not imply any change whatsoever in God—and here let us quote this *hadith* of the Prophet of Islam: 'God was and nothing was with Him; He is now what he was'—likewise the Incarnation does not imply any change because, St Thomas tells us, since the hypostatic union is a relation, '*it is real only in the creature, the Humanity of Jesus. We say in effect that God is united to the creature in the sense that the creature is united to Him, without there being any change in God.*'[34]

---

34. *Summa Theologica*, IIIaP, Q2, A7 ad Im: *haec unio non est in Deo realiter, sed secundum rationem tantum; diciter enim Deus unitas creaturae, ex hoc quod creatura unita est ei, absuque Dei mutatione.* [This union is not really in God, but only in reason, for God is said to be unite to a creature from the fact that the creature is united to God without any change in Him. TRS]

Not wishing to dwell further on this point, we therefore limit ourself to these several reflections and questions concerning the relation between the hypostatic union and the realization of the Self. We would rather see a review of the questions that arise than an exposition of positive solutions. Let us repeat it yet again: the adventurous and risky character of these 'speculations' does not escape us. Furthermore, we clearly see the objection which, from the point of view of the faith, might be raised to the thesis (or hypothesis) that forms the basis of this work, as well as everything that might be required by way of complement, clarification, and refinement. In publishing these reflections we have had no intention other than to bring to the attention of Western thinkers, especially theologians, certain ideas with which they are doubtless unfamiliar, and which, expressed (however imperfectly) in terms of issues that are less alien to them, are capable of providing a mine of nearly inexhaustible reflections. In our exposition we have not had any 'dogmatic' claims. We have not wished to 'convince' anyone. From another angle, we took care to submit our efforts and researches in this particularly delicate domain to an experienced theologian who was kind enough to encourage us to publish them, for which we wish to thank him. Further, as we wrote in our Foreword, scarcely less important than the question of truth is that of opportunity; and in this regard a certain number of signs, several of which we have enumerated, have persuaded us that the time has arrived at which these reflections might be made public. We hope no one will be mistaken as to the spirit in which they were undertaken and conducted.

7

EAST AND WEST

As we near the end of this work, it will be appropriate to review the ground we have covered in an effort to distinguish the elements and method of an analysis which, it must be admitted, has developed rather spontaneously, and to trace the inspiration and guiding force behind the approach. Considering it as a whole, we see that this approach is marked by several symbols of the Supreme Identity, the successive analyses of which constitute the principal steps: the sparkling of the sun on the water, the rope which a man takes for a serpent, a man looking at his own image in a mirror, mental forms seen in sleep, a man who has awakened and whose dream images have vanished.

We have already observed that the first two symbols presume an exterior observer, distinct from the sun and its reflection in the first, and from the rope and the form of a serpent in the second. In the next two symbols, on the contrary, the observer is integral to the symbol, whether it be the man who sees himself in a mirror, or the dreamer. Finally, in the last, the man is perfectly alone, no longer with images or forms, even those produced by himself. The progression is undeniable.

There is also progression in another sense, that of the growing unreality of the exterior world, or more generally of the whole of creation, exterior as well as interior. First, we have the reflection of the sun on the water, which, while not the sun, is nevertheless something real in its own order. The visualized serpent of the second symbol is not pure imagination, it is a rope *taken for* the serpent. We skip the following symbol, that of the man looking at his image in a mirror, for in this regard it is comparable to the first. But in the symbol of the man who dreams, all exterior reality has disappeared;

and in the last, that of the awakened man, there is no mention of any reality, whether exterior or interior; all forms have vanished and only the Self remains.

The progression of symbols seems to embrace more and more closely the mystery of which each symbol conveys or expresses a different aspect; it corresponds both to an ascension and to a deepening. *It is also a series of changes of points of view, each of which remains true at its own level,* an extremely important point which we have noted on several occasions. Symbolic language and an unceasing 're-accommodation' of the eye of the intellect following the variations in points of view, the displacement of levels and the distortion of perspectives which this variation entails—these seem to be the essential elements of the Oriental intellectual approach, as also those by which it differs most profoundly from the West, which latter, if it has discovered perspective in pictorial representation, nevertheless seems to be ignorant of it in intellectual representation,[1] and rarely uses symbolic expression in the expression of the truth. We have intentionally written 'in the expression of' and not 'in the search for' the truth, and here too we grasp one of the most profound differences of the two 'minds'. While the West generally sets out from point zero to advance progressively towards a truth that is to be known from the outside, the East goes from the truth contemplated intuitively to the truth represented, expressed, formulated. And this truth is not regarded as something purely speculative and theoretical, but as That which is and with which one's entire being must be rejoined *so that finally Being and Truth coincide.* The mind of the traditional Orient finds itself in a quasi-natural resonance with certain Gospel formulae, notably with those of St John's Gospel: 'I am the Way, and the Truth, and the Life';[2] or, 'That they all may be one, as thou, Father, in me, and I in thee; that they also may be one in us';[3] or again, 'And you shall know the truth, and the truth

---

1. It is clear that the appearance of perspective in Western pictorial representation expresses the henceforth widespread predominance of the individual point of view; its appearance is the very expression of this predominance.

2. John 14:6.

3. John 17:21.

shall make you free';[4] and, of course, the expression of al-Hallaj: 'I
am the Truth.'

This is why a monk finds himself in natural sympathy and conso-
nance with that form of thought and, so to speak, on the same
plane. By vocation as it were, the monk strives to renew in the West
that 'monastic theology', of which the decline was marked by the
appearance of scholasticism and the universities, this being said
without the least contempt for 'scholastic philosophy' whose forms
of expression, on the contrary, we have constantly borrowed in this
work. Moreover, in the witness of St Thomas himself, who in this
instance cannot be considered suspect, 'scholastic philosophy' itself
is but 'straw'.[5] And yet St Thomas is a giant of true intelligence, profoundly convinced of its requirements. It has been said of him,

> Of all the great doctors, I know of none who is as scornful as he
> is of faith taken as knowledge. If he is measured against his suc-
> cessors, no comparison will more vividly grasp the fading of
> metaphysical ambitions and of the profound intellectualism of
> the Catholic schools since the thirteenth century. Among his
> predecessors, the difference is striking even with St Augustine,
> the fervent apostle of *crede ut intelligas*. Not that St Augustine
> was easily content with earthly obscurities; he strove for the
> Fatherland, the Vision, with all his being; but his scornful judg-
> ment of the knowledge of simple faith does not have the serene
> and definitive tranquility of St Thomas because it is less deliber-
> ately founded in metaphysics. . . . In any case, St Thomas' own
> work is the inculcation of that repugnance which intelligence
> experiences for simple faith: intelligence wishes to see, and noth-
> ing else will ever satisfy it.[6]

If we had to characterize in a brief formula the respective positions
of the modern West, medieval scholasticism, and the Orient with

4. Ibid., 8:32.

5. The reference is to an episode of infused contemplation towards the end of St
Thomas' life, after which he said his writing had come to its end, and he compared
all he had written to straw. TRS

6. Pierre Rousselot, *L'Intellectualisme de Saint Thomas d'Aquin* (Paris: Beau-
chesne, 1936, 3rd ed), chap. VI, §III.

regard to Truth, we would readily say that for the first truth is exterior to intelligence, while for the second it is within intelligence, and for the third that intelligence is in Truth. We ask pardon for whatever is too summary in this rough sketch.

The confusion between symbolic language, on the one hand, and positive and discursive language on the other, is at the root of many errors in the interpretation of Eastern thought. To refer once more to scholastic terminology, we would say that the oriental approach is inclined to follow the schema of the analogy of proportionality: A is to B as C is to D, which Western thought too often interprets as meaning that A equals C.[7] In our analysis of the first symbol, we had occasion to call attention to one such false interpretation, which consists in understanding this symbol to mean that the creature *is* a reflection, whereas the symbol intends only to make us grasp that what the reflection is to the real object, the real and subsistent creature is to God: A is to B as C is to D, and not that C equals A. Other examples of the same confusion could easily be found.

The other principal source of errors and hasty judgments is ignorance of a multitude of possible points of view (this is precisely the meaning of the Sanskrit word *darshana,* from the verbal root *drish,* 'to see', often rendered incorrectly as 'system'), points of view that open onto diverse but *not superimposed* 'perspectives'. As a frequent example of the error resulting from this ignorance we can cite the idealist and subjectivist interpretation of the symbol of the man who dreams. Since the necessary transposition is not effected, it is believed that the cosmos is not exterior to the human individual, the *ego,* while in reality what is involved is the 'point of view' of God

---

7. The theory of the analogy of proportionality is set forth by St Thomas *ex professo* in *De Veritate,* Q2, A11, with an example taken from Aristotle: what sight is for the body, the intellect is for the soul. Further on (Q23, A7), he says that what the pilot is for the ship, the prince is for the city (cf. Bernard Montagnes, *La doctrine de l'analogie de l'être d'apres Saint Thomas d'Aquin,* Louvain: Publications Universitaires, 1963, p78). Speaking more biblically, we would say that what the lamp is for the house, the eye is for the body (Matt. 6:22). In Saint John, all of the 'discourse after the Supper' suggests a somewhat different kind of analogy of proportionality. A is to B what B is to C; what the Father is for the Son, the Son is for the Apostles (cf. John 15:9, 10; 17:18, 21, 22; also 20:21. As the Father hath sent me, I also send you').

who sees and knows all things in Himself as proceeding totally from Himself, as has been explained. Or again, the strictly 'solipsist' interpretation of the symbol of the awakened man for whom all external as well as internal forms have faded, because it is assumed that here, too, it is a question of human individuality, whereas the point of view (using the expression here only in a purely analogical sense) is that of the Infinite outside of which there is nothing just as there is nothing within, because with the Infinite there is neither outside nor inside.

Although we grasp how important it is to consider points of view, it nevertheless seems to have escaped many who have attempted to interpret the thought of the Orient. True, it presumes that we admit the possibility and legitimacy of what we would readily term a displacement of the spiritual focal point, but if such a displacement were impossible, if we were strictly reduced to seeing things from the point of view of human individuality alone (from which moderns seem incapable of escaping other than by adopting a collective point of view, which is of the same order), then the whole mind of the Orient would be mere delusion, not to speak of the Christian mind itself, since, thanks to faith, the Christian is called upon to see all things from the point of view of God. We must not close our eyes to the fact that something of this postulate underlies all 'university philosophy' insofar as its spirit is opposed to that of a 'monastic theology', that is to say, a theology in which a purely theoretical knowledge of a speculative order is never considered an end in itself, but rather as ordered to contemplation, and one might say, *as a simple precondition to interior transfiguration and, in a way, as the schema of the transformation to be effected by the grace of God.*

If we characterize a theology of this type as 'monastic', it is not that we think that the world has or should have less of a monopoly on such a way of thinking than the monk. But if the monk, that is to say each of those who have committed themselves to a monastic way, is a man like others, neither more nor less privileged than others in relation to the intellectual and spiritual transfiguration (*metanoia*) which is normally a requirement imposed on every Christian, the fact remains that the *monastic vocation* supposes at the least a certain aptitude or virtual qualification of this kind, a more distinctive and more pressing call *to consecrate oneself* fully and totally to the 'quest for God', indissolubly linked to the 'quest for self', to realize the Truth in 'the lotus of one's heart'. But today who dares recall men to the ancient lesson of *Ecclesiastes*: 'I have seen all things that are done under the sun, and behold all is vanity, and vexation of spirit'?[8] This is not to say that the efforts of the creature are vanity and chasing the wind, for this would be to see only the efforts of the creature and nothing more, *there where it is necessary to discern and adore the Action of God through man*—'My Father worketh until now; and I work'[9]—and the infallible unrolling of a providential plan.

This doctrine should not be confused with the system of Malebranche for whom secondary causes are simply occasions. A secondary cause is altogether different from an occasional cause. Nevertheless, when we link them, or rather when we become conscious of their link to the providential order, secondary causes, even if free, appear from this more universal point of view as instrumental causes, though without this lessening any of their *relative* reality and autonomy. This is the constant point of view of the Bible where God is said to harden the heart of Pharaoh and chastise Israel by the hand of its enemies, or, conversely, to overcome them when Israel is victorious. It is always the same, however. Blinded by the 'separative' illusion, we attempt to make man's world closed and autonomous, but one which nevertheless continues to exist, as if a room could still retain the light of the sun for a single instant within its closed walls after the shutters had been closed! The world is not 'autonomous', but 'theonomous', God-governed.[10] Whether man in his profane blindness knows this or not, changes nothing. Nothing escapes the sovereign domain of God.

However! We are sometimes tempted to ask if even the Church is not infected with such views. Certainly we see that in adopting her

---

8. Eccl. 1:14

9. John 5:17.

10. We should note that according to the *Advaitic* perspective, which sees the world as not other than *Brahma*, the two expressions are really synonymous; of course, this is not how it is usually understood.

current attitude, the Church tries (not without occasional awkward-ness) to grant certain positive elements of Marxist criticism. But how can one not see that the most representative and lively of the rising generations are in violent reaction against the 'positivism' and the 'economism' of their elders—and also against a certain blind prejudice? If the closing twentieth century has been that of 'social-ization' and 'technicization', many corroborating indications lead us to think that the first century of the third millennium may be, at least for some, of whom the number is growing, that of the *quest for lost identity*. Is it not precisely this which explains why contempo-rary young people with their 'hunger for the absolute' (which, although too often mixed with elements that are more than suspect, is undeniably characteristic of them), turn so readily towards the non-Christian East to try to discover what Christianity no longer, or seems no longer, to offer them? Is not one of the most notable ser-vices which the Orient could render Christianity today, to oblige it to return to its own center instead of seeming to wish to dilute its identity in a hollow and vacuous world where all interiority, all sol-itude, all silence, all recollection, have been banished?

We can no longer write that 'the monk is no longer at the level of *māyā*,' nor, 'if he acts in the world of *māyā*, it is as the Self,'[11] and we admit that we do not understand how one could write such things. Considering only the monks of today, they seem no less 'disillu-sioned' than their contemporaries living in the world. It would really be too simple and too convenient if the fact of living within a monastic community after having made one's vows, sufficed to assure the quality of being 'delivered in life'! The monastic way is a way; it is not *the* Way. Even less is it the goal. The Lord is the Way. There is no other. The essence of Christianity, and therefore of Christian monasticism, is comprised in three words: identification with Christ. All the rest is of trifling importance. And thus we have Christocentrism, as Vatican II has recalled most opportunely (but only on the level of 'economy', as our Orthodox brethren would

---

11. Jules Monchanin and Henri Le Saux, *Ermites du Saccidananda: un Essai d'Integration Chretien de la Tradition Monastique de l'Inde* ['a Christian attempt to interpret the monastic tradition of India'] (Paris: Casterman, 1956), p 63.

say), that is, in regard to all 'secondary devotions'. If from the plane of 'economy' we pass to that of 'theology', then a 'patrocentrism' and a 'pneumatocentrism' must be associated with this 'Christocentrism', God being like an infinite Sphere with three distinct centers which nevertheless coincide, if we may so phrase it.

That said, we are firmly convinced that Christian monasticism has a primary rôle to play, both in the spiritual renewal of Christianity itself and in bringing together Christianity and the East, two things which, despite those who seem to see only opposition and mutual exclusion everywhere, appear to be closely linked in actuality. This presumes first of all that monasticism itself is renewed. We do not say that it 'reform itself.' The exterior forms granted so much consideration in the West, even and perhaps especially by monasticism, are of slight importance. The 'flesh' and the 'letter' are of little use,[12] and as Abbot Monchanin loved to say, 'The Spirit is metamorphic.' Ramana Maharshi once made the following remark, apt to provoke monks to 'discernment', a monastic virtue if ever there was one! To someone who asked him if he should understand renunciation to mean becoming a monk, Maharshi responded,

> When you live in the world, you think 'I live in the world'; and when you become a monk, you think 'I live as a monk'. What do you gain by this change?

This does not mean that for the one who is called it is a matter of indifference whether or not he embraces the monastic life, but rather that every 'condition', even that of monasticism, must be (spiritually) surpassed, *because the true vocation of man is the Infinite*. St John of the Cross advised monks to live in the monastery 'as not being there'. 'If you would become everything, strive to become nothing in nothing.'[13]

The monk who tries to become what his name signifies is entirely turned towards the Unique just as the heliotrope is turned towards the sun. In a letter addressed to the Abbot General of the Trappists (OCSO), Paul VI wrote:

12. Cf. John 6:63 [64 in the Douay Version TRS]
13. John of the Cross, *Montée du Carmel*, p 86.

In a way, God Himself is established at the center of the monk's life, and occupies it completely. As St Theodore the Studite said, he looks towards God, is passionate for God alone, devoted to God alone. . . . There, without any doubt, is the aim of monastic life.[14]

He is a monk who has realized with his entire being that *Unam est necessarium* [the one thing is necessary], that is to say, not simply that few things, or even one alone, suffice to assure one's existence, but that what is necessary is *Being-One*. The monk is the man of Unity, that is, the man of the Spirit. Will it be said that he has chosen the better part? No. A part, even if the best, is not sufficient for him; like the little Thérèse, he 'chooses all'.[15] This is what makes him a monk.

It will no doubt be said that we have spoken very little about love, and some people will be scandalized, for is it not by charity that we go to God? Certainly, but *amor ipse est intellectus* [love itself is intellect]; and is to speak of unity anything other than to speak of charity? Also, if it is by love that one *goes* to God, it is by the intelligence that He is *possessed*. Let us again quote Fr Rousselot:

Which faculty is nobler, intelligence or will? By what power does the created being possess the Infinite, by the intelligence or by the will? These are problems which the Scholastics posed explicitly, and while their responses to these questions classified them as intellectualists or voluntarists, they were also eminently characteristic of their systems, *because for them the responses decided the nature of God on whom all depends*. In Scholasticism there is a principal question, one could almost say a unique question,

14. Letter of Paul VI of December 8, 1968.

15. One day Leonie, thinking she was too big to play with dolls, came to both of us with a basket filled with dresses and pretty scraps intended to make more; her doll was lying on the top. 'Help yourselves, my little sisters,' she said, 'choose, I give you all of this.' Céline put out her hand and took a small package of braid which she liked. After a moment of reflection, I put my hand forward saying: 'I *choose everything*! and I took the basket with no more ado. . . . *This little feature of my childhood is the resumé of my whole life* [emphasis added]. Thérèse of Liseux, *Manuscrits Autobiographiques* (Paris: Livre de Vie, 1966), p38.

which is that of the conquest of being.[16] It is by approaching medieval thinkers from this perspective that we understand them as they were.[17]

---

16. 'Conquest" is an unfortunate word choice, but given that a thoroughly traditional epistemology was unavailable to Fr Rousselot, it is understandable that this manner of expression was used. TRS

17. Rousselot, *L'Intellectualisme de Saint Thomas d'Aquin*, Introduction (emphasis added).

CONCLUSION

HAVING REVIEWED the several elements analyzed in the course of this work, are we now able to come to a real conclusion? If we mean by this a definitive conclusion, it would be quite presumptuous to make such a claim. We are personally convinced that a 'Christian non-dualism', to borrow Vladimir Lossky's expression already quoted in the Foreword, is not to be dismissed *on the basis of the Faith*, but we do not flatter ourself that our account has succeeded in convincing every honest reader. Conversely, should we admit that we do not see how the opposite is to be proved? All that can be said is that nowhere does Scripture make the slightest allusion to anything of this kind, at least explicitly,[1] but is this sufficient reason to discard it? Scripture does not say everything and, moreover, does not need to. It teaches us only what is necessary for our salvation.

St Thomas Aquinas teaches that integral doctrine is not circumscribed within the limits of 'what is written', but that by reason of its excellence (*propter excellentiam*), not only is Christ's teaching not totally contained in the written accounts, but cannot be so contained (*litteris comprehendi non potest*).[2] To support his thesis, he cites the last verse of the *Gospel according to St John*:

> But there are also many other things which Jesus did; which, if they were written every one, the world itself, I think, could not contain the books that should be written.

---

1. There are in fact numerous passages especially in the Gospel of St John, and even in the Synoptic Gospels and Pauline Epistles, which, as the author recognizes, if not explicit in this regard nevertheless clearly imply an esoteric meaning and point to the possibility of metaphysical realization. TRS

2. *Summa Theologica*, IIIaP, Q42, to which we will refer in all that follows. Also cf. *IV Sent. 23*, I,I: *Illa enim praecipue curaverunt evangelistae tradere ad salutis necessitatem . . . pertinent* (The first concern of the Evangelists was to transmit all that pertains to the necessity of salvation).

Let us note in passing how strange it is that such an apparently extravagant passage, even allowing for 'oriental exaggeration', receives so little attention.

According to St Thomas, one of the reasons why Christ in his wisdom did not will to record his teaching in writing was 'so that men should not think that His doctrine comprised nothing other than the written accounts might contain' (*nihil aliud de ejus doctrina homines aestimarent quam quod scriptura contineret*). St Thomas' thinking is therefore perfectly clear; for him there was no doubt whatsoever that the oral and 'factual' teaching of Christ went greatly beyond what the writings could contain. But he did not stop there, for he held that even in his oral teaching Christ did not reveal either to the multitudes or even to his disciples (*nec etiam discipulis*) the full depths of His wisdom (*omnia profunda suae sapientiae*), but only what he judged suitable for communication to them (*quodcumque dignum duxit*). St Thomas held further that even this latter was not understood by everyone (*licet non ab omnibus intelligeretur*). After such statements, we cannot understand why some persist in presenting St Thomas, a man who had in such high degree the sense and the understanding of mystery, as a rationalist before the fact.

Certainly it would be a poor argument for St Thomas' judgment to take it as a pretext for accepting just any doctrine or pseudo-esoteric claim, but at least it invites us not to reject *a priori* what we do not find contained in the Scriptures, of course on condition that it does not contradict revelation as this is interpreted by the authentic teaching of the magisterium.

We have already had occasion to note that here everything, or nearly everything, revolves around the notion of person. From the first centuries of Christianity, theological reflection concerning revelation felt constrained to distinguish persons and substance in God in its effort to explain the Trinitarian Mystery rationally. Much later this effort led the Western Church to define the divine Persons as 'subsistent relations'. The later elaboration of the general idea of person by profane philosophy is largely indebted to this properly theological explication, notably as regards the relational structure of the person. This relational—and thus, in this sense, 'relative'—

character of the person is, as will have been noted, a capital element in our research, particularly as regards the manner in which God as Creator may be conceived. As we have had occasion to recall, the creature-Creator relation is real only from the point of view of the creature who, moreover, is defined by it. One immediate result of this relational character, inherent in the creature as such, is that the human notion of a (uni-) personal God *relative to creation,* that is to say the idea that we 'naturally' form of God, can only be provisional, a sort of concession to our mental weakness.[3] It is *we* who are relative to God and are thereby constituted as 'persons'. Here the profound connection linking the two questions of Moses on Mt Horeb, 'Who am I?' and 'What is thy Name?' appears in full clarity, and we could say that the revelation of our true identity in its varying degrees of profundity (because, as we have seen, there are degrees of identity as there are degrees of unity), is linked to the various divine Names. It is regrettable that this conception, familiar to the lofty Tradition of Israel, seems to be totally neglected by Christians who nevertheless find their true supernatural identity in the divine Name Jesus Christ.

It seems to us that understood in this way, this rather pedagogically provisional character of the idea of a God who is personal in relation to the creature, or of a divine 'Thou', should permit Christians, especially theologians, to understand and admit the non-dualist understanding of the 'illusory' nature of 'God-the-producer-of-beings' (*Brahmā*)—given the necessary specifications and adjustments. Does it not go without saying that the essential Mystery infinitely transcends the 'Face' of God-as-Creator?

O Depth of riches, how incomprehensible you are! So long as I conceive a creator creating, I am still on this side of the wall of paradise. And so long as I imagine a creatable creator, I have not yet entered, but am at the wall. *But when I see You as absolute infinity, for whom neither the name of creating creator nor that of*

---

3. *Deus est vox relativa* (Newton), cited in Léonid Chrol, *Alpha et Omega* (Montauban, chez l'auteur, 1967), p43.

*creatable creator is suitable, then I begin to see You without veils,
and to enter the garden of delights.*[4]

In the same order of ideas, let us call attention to a certain insufficiency of contemporary theological formulations concerning what
is commonly designated the 'exterior missions', that is the sending
forth of the Word and the Spirit to the world. If we speak here of
insufficiency—it would be better to speak of 'incompleteness'—it is
not that the expression is false, but only that it presupposes and
entails a *representation*, no doubt convenient and provisionally sufficient, but misleading, and ultimately deceptive as regards the Real.
It is in fact impossible that God go out of Himself. There can be no
reciprocity, real reciprocity, between Man and God *except in the Son,
in the bosom of the Trinity, in the interior of the eternal relation of the
Son to the Father.* It is in order that man might be raised to this point
that the Father sent his Son and his Spirit. It is therefore perfectly
legitimate to speak of 'exterior missions' from the human point of
view (in doing which we are only conforming to the language of the
Bible), since it is in this way that in fact they appear to man. But this
point of view is insufficient and demands completion by the 'point
of view of God' which, as we have said, always implies a reversal of
perspectives. What is more, this last point of view must be surpassed
in its turn, *because it is impossible that anything 'be introduced'* into
God which is not already there. 'He chose us in Him (Christ) *before
the foundation of the world*,'[5] and 'no man hath ascended into
heaven, but he that descended from heaven, the Son of man who is
in heaven.'[6] However, and let us say this again, when the latter point
of view is adopted it is necessary to transpose beings 'outside' their
creaturely condition and to consider them in the eternal Word, 'in
the condition of God'.

A related idea of no less importance is that of *Aseity.*[7] We have

---

4. Nicolas of Cusa, *Traité de la Vision de Dieu*, trans. Edmond Vansteenberghe
(Louvain: Éditions du Museum Lessianum, 1925), chap. xii.
5. Eph. 1:4.
6. John 3:14.
7. This idea should not be confused with the contradictory Cartesian idea of a
God who is *causa sui* [His own cause].

already said—but perhaps some did not grasp the full import of the remark at the time—that this idea corresponds as precisely as possible, taking into account the diversity of the points of view, to what Hinduism designates as *Reality*. The Reality of non-dualism should thus not be identified with what the same word designates in Western philosophical terminology. *The Infinite alone being from-Itself (à-Se) (or, we repeat, 'non ab alio'* [not from another]) *the identification of the concept of Reality with that of Aseity explains why, in the view of the non-dualist, it is the Infinite which is The Reality.* The finite has no existence except insofar as we consider it 'in itself' and *separatively,* a consideration which can only be illusory in regard to the Infinite. We can present these things another way. Since every distinction implies a limitation, and God must obviously be considered unlimited in His essential Mystery, it follows that the world can be distinguished from Him *only at a certain level of reality,* precisely where 'creation', and therefore also 'the Creator', is real. *Fundamentally, the illusion of 'separativity' is inherent in the creaturely condition.*[8]

We have also noted the contemporary Western confusion between *aseity* (to be by means of oneself, not to owe one's existence to any other, *ab alio*) and *substantiality* (to subsist in oneself, as against being 'accidental'). It seems to us that here we have an important observation that can be used to parry the reproach of a 'desubstantialization' of the world, as if the existence of a divine and transcendent Being implied the 'non-essentiality of man's nature' (to borrow Marx's expression once again).

We hope that the reader now understands the necessity for both the task of translation and for *true* equivalents, which latter need we have already mentioned, notably in connection with the current rendering of *Ātmā* by 'soul'. If we would truly enter into the thought of non-dualist Hinduism so disorienting for a Westerner, we must first of all assimilate that mentality and become capable of envisaging

8. This is not to say that the creature must not endeavor to liberate himself therefrom. Cf. Thomas à Kempis, *The Imitation of Christ*, L.I, chap. III, v.10: *Cui omnia unam sunt, et omnia ad unam trahit, et omnium in uno videt, potest stabilis corde esse, et in Deo pacificus permanere* (He for whom all things are one, who leads all things to unity, and sees all things in unity, he can be unruffled in heart and remain peaceful in God.)

things in terms of different issues, and of admitting the possibility and legitimacy of a true renewal of our perspective. What is involved is a kind of 'gymnastic', 'a laying bare', that is in every way salutary, and that can be a powerful aid for ourselves to enter more deeply into our own Revelation (if one may so speak) and our own mystery, though doubtless everyone is not equally prepared for this.

It seems to us that after these clarifications, the accusation of pantheistic monism brought against the Hindu doctrine of non-dualism must fall away of itself, at least if we do not wish to make of 'God' a limited and simplistic idea, and if we are willing to 'transcend current received theism', to borrow the expression of Dewey quoted in the first chapter. How can a doctrine that, insofar as possible, aims at *infinite* and therefore total and unique Reality, in regard to Which all (*pan*) disappears including the 'creator-God' himself (*theos*), be characterized as pantheism? It would be better to speak of 'a-theism' (in the sense in which the Romans characterized the first Christians as 'atheists') and of 'a-cosmism', as is sometimes done, but always in forgetfulness that partial points of view that have been surpassed do not thereby become false, even if they must be said to be insufficient. All these points of view are harmoniously integrated and rediscovered in the total Truth. Let us not confuse a radical 'apophaticism', even if pushed to the extreme limits of possibility, namely the spirit of negative theology— but here we have something other than theology—with the spirit of negation which is only its satanic parody, even if the latter sometimes produces *formulations* which seem identical. This is one of the reasons why we have alluded to the necessity for a true 'discernment of spirits'. The reader can now fully understand what we wish to say thereby. Let us thus guard against committing that 'sin against the Spirit' of which it has been said that 'it shall not be forgiven ... neither in this world, nor in the world to come,'[9] by thoughtlessly casting the suspicion of 'Satanism' on doctrines and spiritual approaches simply because these are far removed from our habitual ways of perceiving and acting; borrowing the words of John Paul II already cited, let us

9. Matt. 12:31–32 [Both the Douay and Authorized Versions render 'sin' as 'blasphemy'. TRS]

rather be attentive to 'the Spirit of Truth working beyond the visible frontiers of the Mystical Body.'

Similarly can the reader, if he has followed us this far, understand why despite common usage we have judged it preferable to speak of the Infinite rather than the Absolute? We have just said it: from the point of view of the infinite and *unique* Reality—unique because Infinite—but only from this point of view, all fades away and disappears (this is the glance of *Shiva* which reduces all to ashes), not by 'annihilation', not in losing its veritable identity, *but in finding Itself infinitely*, because there is nothing to be had, except as the effect of illusion and 'separativity', outside the Infinite where all is necessarily found, but not as Its parts. We are certain that no one will charge this proposition with 'monism' or 'pantheism'. Would it be the same if, instead of the Infinite, we spoke of the Absolute?

We said above that not everyone was prepared for these incessant interior reversals which are like a gymnastic and without which it is not possible to enter into the spirit of *advaita-vāda*, so strange to the Western mind. It is not a question of 'intelligence' in the ordinary sense of the term. It may even be asked if the generally rather unilateral formation (in the sense in which scientific thinking is necessarily 'monovalent') of intellectuals prepares them well for this kind of 'exercise'.[10] No doubt certain special aptitudes are necessary which, naturally, are not found in everyone. However that may be, it would be extremely dangerous for anyone who, for one reason or another, might be unsuited for this constant labor of 'recovery', incessant changes of points of view, reversal of perspectives, perpetual 're-accommodations' of the intellectual eye, to seize non-dualist formulations and attempt to feed off them.

---

10. In this order of ideas it must be noted also that of all attachments, that of which the consequences are the most to be feared is that of attachment to one's intelligence. 'Those who are absorbed in the senses remain [in transmigration] for ten *manvantaras* [cosmic cycles]; those who are absorbed in the elements remain there for a hundred *manvantaras*; those who are absorbed in the *ahankāra* remain there for a thousand *manvantaras*; those who are absorbed in the *buddhi* (the intellectual faculty) remain there for ten thousand *manvantaras* (cited by René Allar, *La Prasna Upanishad. et son commentaire par Shankarāchārya*, *Études Traditionnelles* 1961, p290).

We do not see what more we might add without repetition. We will therefore come to an end, certain that the reader has in hand all the elements necessary for an evaluation. As for ourself, we will say unequivocally that after more than forty years of intellectual reflection on this doctrine, having allowed it to impregnate us more and more profoundly, we have found nothing that has seemed incompatible with our full and complete faith in the Christian Revelation. However, we do not have the authority to make final judgments in these matters, and we now leave the last word to judges of greater competence and authority.

LaVergne, TN USA
09 January 2011
211698LV00004B/109/A